HISPANICS
IN U.S. HISTORY

THROUGH 1865

Quercus Volume A

Senior Consultant
Frank de Varona, *Associate Superintendent*
Bureau of Education
Dade County Public Schools
Miami, Florida

Consultants
Yolanda Quintanilla-Finley, *Title VII Project Specialist*
in Sheltered English
Rowland Unified School District
Rowland Heights, California

Alice S. Gaines, *Learning Consultant/Special Education*
Burlington County School District
Mt. Holly, New Jersey

Editorial Assistance
by Editorial Options, Inc.

QUERCUS
A Division of
Globe Book Company
Englewood Cliffs, New Jersey

Photo Acknowledgments

Introduction p. 3: Gary S. Tong. **Lesson 1** pp. 5: The Granger Collection; 6: Culver Pictures; 7: Culver Pictures. **Lesson 2** pp. 9: The Granger Collection; 11: Culver Pictures. **Lesson 3** pp. 13: Gary S. Tong; 14: Biblioteca Nacional, Madrid/Laurie Platt Winfrey; 15: Courtesy Department Library Services, American Museum of Natural History. **Lesson 4** pp. 17: Hispanic Society of America; 18: The American Museum of Natural History; 19: The Granger Collection. **Review 1** p. 21: Gary S. Tong. **Lesson 5** pp. 23: Gary S. Tong; 24: Florida State Archives; 25: Florida State Archives. **Lesson 6** pp. 27: Gary S. Tong; 28: F.B. Grunzweig/Photo Researchers; 29: Courtesy Museum of New Mexico. **Lesson 7** pp. 31: U.T. Institute of Texan Culture, San Antonio; 32: Gary S. Tong; 33: U.T. Institute of Texan Culture, San Antonio. **Lesson 8** pp. 35: Gary S. Tong; 36: The Granger Collection; 37: California Section, California State Library. **Review 2** p. 39: Gary S. Tong. **Lesson 9** pp. 41: Gary S. Tong; 42: Cover to Cover, Inc.; 43: The Historic New Orleans Collection. **Lesson 10** pp. 45: Karsh, Ottawa, Courtesy of Arizona Historical Society Library; 47: Museo Nacional de Historica/Laurie Platt Winfrey. **Lesson 11** pp. 49: Louisiana State Library; 50: Museo Nacional de Historica/Laurie Platt Winfrey; 51: Artist Miranda/Laurie Platt Winfrey. **Lesson 12** pp. 53: Florida State Archives; 54: Cover to Cover, Inc.; 55: Florida State Archives. **Lesson 13** pp. 57: Florida State Archives; 58: Culver Pictures. **Review 3** p. 61: Gary S. Tong. **Lesson 14** pp. 63: Culver Pictures; 64: The Granger Collection; 65: Museum of New Mexico. **Lesson 15** pp. 67: Florida State Archives; 68: Gary S. Tong; 69: Florida State Archives. **Lesson 16** pp. 71: Culver Pictures; 72: Gary S. Tong. **Lesson 17** pp. 75: U.T. Institute of Texan Culture, San Antonio; 76: Gary S. Tong; 77: Texas State Capitol, Austin, Texas. **Lesson 18** pp. 79: Library of Congress; 80: Gary S. Tong. **Lesson 19** pp. 83: Culver Pictures; 84: Gary S. Tong; 85: The Granger Collection; **Review 4** p. 87: Cover to Cover, Inc.

Front Cover, clockwise: Sor Juana Inés de la Cruz, Hernando de Soto, María Josefa Ortiz de Domínguez, David Farragut
Cover art: David Dircks
Photo research: Omni-Photo Communications, Inc.

Printed in the United States of America
10 9 8 7 6 5 4 3 2 1
ISBN: 1-55675-554-6

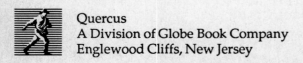

Quercus
A Division of Globe Book Company
Englewood Cliffs, New Jersey

CONTENTS

CONTENTS *(continued)*

INTRODUCTION

Hispanic Americans are a very important part of America's past, present, and future. We are going to learn about the exciting history of Hispanic Americans. But first we need to understand what the word Hispanic means. The word <u>Hispanic</u> means "a person whose language and traditions come from a country where Spanish is spoken." Many Spanish-speaking people live in countries that are in Central America and South America. These countries are very far from Spain.

How did these people in countries so far from Spain become Spanish-speaking? To answer that question, we have to go back to the 1400s. At that time, the first explorers came from Spain to the "New World." The "New World" was South America, Central America, and North America.

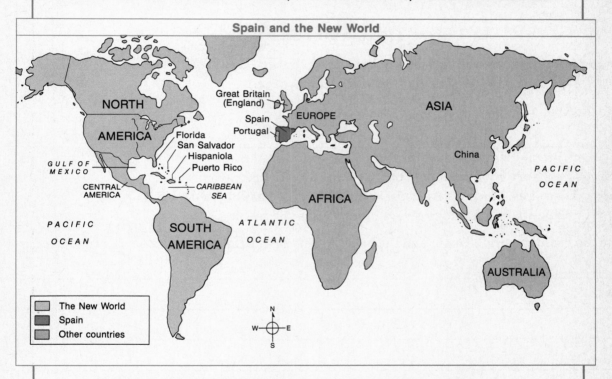

Spain and the New World

Let's look at the map now. Point to Spain. Now find South America, Central America, and North America. You can see that explorers had to cross the Atlantic Ocean in order to come to the New World.

Why did Spanish explorers come to the New World? Where did the Spanish settle in the New World? How did the Spanish way of life change the lives of the Native Americans who lived in the New World? What part did Hispanics play in the Revolutionary War and the Civil War? You will find the answers to these and many more interesting questions as you read Volume A.

SPAIN AND THE NEW WORLD

LEARN NEW WORDS

Say each word. Write the word in the sentence.

goods (GOODZ)

merchant (MUR-chunt)

route (ROOT)

island (EYE-lund)

1. The trader sold cloth, food, and other _____ .

2. A trader who buys and sells goods is a _____ .

3. A path to travel by land or water is a _____ .

4. Because Cuba has water on all sides it is called an _____ .

LEARN A SKILL: Using Titles and Headings

The **title** tells what the reading will be about. Find the title "Spain and the New World." It is in big, dark letters at the top of this page.

Write the title.

_____

Readings in history books are often broken into parts. Before each part is a **heading**. Like titles, headings are in dark, big letters. The headings tell what the part will be about. Headings give the main ideas of a reading.

Write the headings from "Spain and the New World" on the lines below.

_____

_____

_____

_____

_____

MAKE PREDICTIONS

Read the title and headings. Use them to make predictions.

Put a (✔) mark next to the things you think you will learn about.

_____ why traders wanted to get to Asia

_____ what idea Columbus had

_____ why Columbus asked for help

_____ Columbus's life as a young boy

_____ Columbus in the "New World"

_____ why Columbus was a hero

OBJECTIVE: **Find out why people from Spain came to the "New World."**

TIP: **The title and headings will help you.**

Traders Want to Get to Asia

1. Picture this. It is the year 1450. You are a trader living in **Europe**. You spend most of your time buying and selling **goods** at trade fairs. During the 1400s, **merchants** came to trade fairs from many countries.

2. While you are buying and selling goods at trade fairs, you hear news about other parts of the world. You hear that gold, fine silks, and spices can be found in **Asia**.

3. Merchants say land **routes** to Asia are controlled by traders from the Middle East. You could be killed if you tried to get to Asia over these land routes.

 REREAD Where did merchants say gold, silks, and spices could be found?

Christopher Columbus Has an Idea

4. You want to find another way to get to Asia. You think about going by water. But no one has tried this before.

5. Meanwhile, a seaman from Italy, named Christopher Columbus, liked this idea. He wanted to go to Asia to find gold, silks, and spices. He thought that if he sailed west from Europe, he would find a shorter route to Asia.

 REVIEW Why did Columbus want to go to Asia? Hint: The second sentence in paragraph 5 will tell you.

▲ Christopher Columbus sailed to the "New World" in 1492.

Columbus Asks for Help

6. Columbus needed many things for his trip. He needed money to buy food, supplies, and ships. Columbus asked leaders of many countries to help him out, but they would not. They thought his idea was wrong. No one had ever tried going west to Asia by water.

7. Finally, in 1492, Queen Isabella of **Spain** gave Columbus some of the money he needed. With that money and more that he borrowed, Columbus bought three ships. The ships were called the *Niña*, the *Pinta*, and the *Santa María*. Columbus also used the money to buy food and supplies and to pay his men.

Columbus Reaches the "New World"

8. Columbus's trip across the **ocean** took two months. Columbus left Spain on August 3, 1492. He headed west with three ships and 90 men. How excited the sailors on the *Pinta* must

have been when they saw land. Columbus and his men landed on October 12, 1492.

9. Columbus landed on some **islands**. Today these islands are called the Bahama Islands. He named the island on which he landed **San Salvador**. Columbus had not landed in Asia. The place where Columbus landed came to be called the **"New World."**

10. Columbus then sailed on to the islands of Cuba and **Hispaniola** (his-pun-YOH-luh). He did see gold worn by the **Native Americans**, the people already living in the New World. He did not find spices or fine silks.

LOOK

Look at the map on page 3. Draw in Columbus's route west (left) from Palos, Spain to San Salvador. Did Columbus find a shorter route to Asia?

Columbus Is a Hero

11. Columbus was called a hero in Spain. The news spread fast that he had found a New World. Queen Isabella was very pleased. Queen Isabella made Columbus "Admiral of the Ocean Sea."

12. Columbus made three more trips to the New World. Many of the people Columbus brought with him from Spain stayed in the New World. In all his trips, Columbus never found gold, fine silks, or spices to trade. Instead, he found a New World for Spain.

TALK

Do you think you would try to join Christopher Columbus on one of his trips to the New World? Why? Talk about it with your classmates.

13. In what ways would history change because of Columbus's discovery? The history of the New World would be changed forever. Spain would soon control millions of square miles of land in the New World. People who had lived in the New World would now be under the control of Spain. Many people would come from Spain to live in the New World.

▲ The *Santa María* was the largest of the three ships. Columbus sailed the *Santa María* himself.

UNDERSTANDING WHAT YOU HAVE READ

Find the correct answer to each question. Circle the letter.

1. Why did traders want to get to Asia?
   a. to find new places to live
   b. to buy gold, spices, and silks
   c. to find new animals and plants

2. What was Columbus's idea?
   a. a faster ship would get him to Asia
   b. a new land route would get him to Asia
   c. sailing west would get him to Asia

3. Who gave Columbus some of the money he needed?
   a. the King of Italy
   b. the leaders of many countries
   c. Queen Isabella of Spain

4. In what year did Columbus first come to the New World?
   a. 1900
   b. 1492
   c. 1450

5. Why did Columbus become a hero in Spain?
   a. for being a good seaman
   b. for finding a New World for Spain
   c. for taking people to the New World

Spotlight on People: Queen Isabella of Spain

What was Queen Isabella like? Queen Isabella of Spain was strong-willed and powerful. She did not agree with people who thought that Columbus's plan would not work. She decided he was right.

Queen Isabella believed strongly in the Roman Catholic **religion**. Queen Isabella forced everyone to become Christian or leave Spain. She made a plan with Columbus. In this plan, Isabella said that all people living on lands owned by Spain would have to become Christians. Otherwise, these people would have to leave the Spanish lands.

▲ Queen Isabella hears Columbus's plan.

EXPLORERS FROM SPAIN

LEARN NEW WORDS

Say each word. Write the word in the sentence.

explorer (ik-SPLOR-ur)

conquer (KAHN-kur)

claim (KLAYM)

1. A person who travels to new lands is called an _____ .

2. To fight and win control over a country is to _____ it.

3. When you say you own something, it means you _____ it.

LEARN A SKILL: Using Charts

On a **chart** things are grouped together. The groups are listed in rows and in columns. To read a chart, you read across (→) a row and down (↓) a column. Charts help you to look up and compare facts quickly.

> **Hint:**
> Look across (→) a row and down (↓) a column.

Read the title of the chart on page 10. The title will tell you what you can find out from the chart. To look up something on this chart, you will have to read down (↓) and look across (→).

Put a (✔) mark next to your answers.

1. How many explorers are listed on the chart?
   _____ 1
   _____ 4
   _____ 5

2. Which explorer discovered Florida?
   _____ Piñeda
   _____ Coronado
   _____ Ponce de León

3. Which explorer went to the Grand Canyon?
   _____ Coronado
   _____ Piñeda
   _____ Cabrillo

4. Did the chart help you find out what you wanted to know quickly?
   _____ yes
   _____ no

MAKE PREDICTIONS

Read the title and headings. Use them to make predictions.

Put a (✔) mark next to the things you think you will learn about.

_____ who came to the New World

_____ who explored the coasts

_____ who searched for gold

_____ what gold is used for

_____ who explored the Pacific coast

_____ fishing in the Pacific Ocean

OBJECTIVE: **Read to find out the names of explorers from Spain who first came to North America.**

TIP: **The chart will help you.**

Explorers Come to the New World

1. When Columbus returned from the New World, he told about what he had seen there. Many **explorers** were excited by Columbus's news. They wanted to see what he had seen. They wondered what other surprises they might find in the New World. Explorers from Spain were called **conquistadores** (kon-KEES-tah-dor-ehs), which means "people who **conquer**."

2. Many conquistadores decided to come to the New World. Conquistadores came because they wanted to conquer new lands. They wanted to find great riches, such as gold, silver, and jewels.

3. Other people came to the New World. These people were **missionaries**. Missionaries were sent from Spain to the New World by the Catholic Church. They were sent to teach the Christian religion to the **Native Americans**.

 REREAD Give two reasons why people from Spain came to the New World.

4. One of the first explorers in the New World was Juan Ponce de León (PON-seh deh leh-OHN). Ponce de León was probably the first explorer known to land on North America. He had been with Columbus on his second trip. Ponce de León stayed in the New World to explore the land on his own. In the year 1508, he discovered gold on the island of Puerto Rico. From Puerto Rico, he sailed northwest. In 1513, he discovered the beautiful land which he called "La Florida."

▲ Ponce de León claimed Florida for Spain.

Ponce de León explored much of southern Florida. He decided to **claim** Florida for Spain.

Exploring Along the Coasts

5. Other Spanish explorers came to the New World. They sailed along the **coasts**. The coast is the land next to the ocean. In the year 1519, Alonso Alvarez de Piñeda (deh pee-NEH-dah) sailed from Hispaniola, along the coast of the Gulf of Mexico. Piñeda made many important discoveries. He was the first explorer to find out that Florida was part of North America. Piñeda also was the first **European** to see the Mississippi River.

 LOOK Look at the map on page 7. Trace with your finger the route that Ponce de León took from Puerto Rico to Florida.

The Search for Gold Begins

6. In 1527, another Spanish explorer, Pánfilo de Narváez (deh-nahr-VAH-es), heard stories about gold to the north of Florida. He left his ships on the Florida coast. He and his men marched inland, but they did not find gold. When they returned to the coast, their ships were gone. Narváez's men had to make small boats. They tried to sail along the Gulf of Mexico. Most of the men died. Others were taken as prisoners by Native Americans. Cabeza de Vaca (deh VAH-kah), a survivor of Narváez's 1527 expedition, traveled west through Texas and into Mexico.

REVIEW Did Narváez and his men find what they were looking for?

7. Another one of Narváez's men was Estevanico (es-teh-vah-NEE-koh), a Black slave. He traveled to the southwestern part of North America. Native Americans told him about the **"Seven Cities of Gold."** Estevanico searched for the cities. He traveled with Father Marco de Niza (deh NEE-sah). Estevanico died while looking for the "Seven Cities of Gold". But Father Marco de Niza told other explorers what he had seen and heard.

8. Who did de Niza tell about the "Seven Cities of Gold"? He told an explorer named Francisco Vásquez de Coronado (deh kor-uh-NAHD-oh). In the year 1540, Coronado had reached the Southwest. Coronado searched for the "Seven Cities of Gold," but he never found them. His men were the first Europeans to see the Grand Canyon. They traveled east to the land now called Kansas. Coronado claimed all the land he saw in the New World for Spain.

TALK Imagine you are traveling with Coronado. Are you happy or unhappy with what you find? Why? Discuss your answer with your classmates.

Explorers Reach the Pacific Coast

9. In the year 1542, an explorer named Juan Rodríguez Cabrillo (kah-BREE-yoh) sailed along the Pacific coast. He and his men were probably the first Europeans to see what is now called the California coast. Some of Cabrillo's men sailed north to present-day Oregon. They were led by an explorer named Bartolomé Ferrelo (feh-REH-loh).

EARLY SPANISH EXPLORERS IN AMERICA

Explorer	Land Explored	Discovery
Ponce de León	Florida	First European to come to North America
Piñeda	Coast of the Gulf of Mexico	First European to reach Mississippi River
Coronado	Southwest North America	Explored Grand Canyon
Cabrillo	Pacific Coast	First European to see coast of California

▲ This chart shows discoveries made by early explorers from Spain. Test yourself: Which explorer was the first to see the coast of California?

CHECK THE OBJECTIVE: **Write down in your notebook the name of one explorer from Spain who came to North America. Tell what land he explored.**

AFTER YOU READ

Lesson **2**

UNDERSTANDING WHAT YOU HAVE READ

Read the words in the box. Write the word that completes each sentence.

Ponce de León	explorers
missionaries	Pacific coast

1. Most _____ came to the New World to look for gold.

2. The _____ wanted to teach the Christian religion to the people of the New World.

3. _____ discovered Florida and claimed it for Spain.

4. Explorers of the _____ saw the coasts of California and Oregon.

Spotlight on People: Hernando de Soto

Hernando de Soto (deh SOH-toh) was another famous explorer from Spain. De Soto left Spain when he was 14 years old to sail to the New World. He spent the next 20 years of his life exploring Central America and South America. (Central America is the land between North and South America.)

In 1539, de Soto met Juan Ortiz. Ortiz had been with Narváez in Florida. He told de Soto about rich land to the north.

De Soto and his men traveled north with Ortiz. They went as far north as where Georgia and North Carolina are today. They crossed the Smokey Mountains and traveled west as far as the Mississippi River.

In the year 1542, de Soto died of a fever. He had never found gold. But he did explore the southeastern part of America.

▲ De Soto and his men meet Native Americans near the Mississippi River.

SPANISH EXPLORERS IN MEXICO AND PERU

LEARN NEW WORDS

Say each word. Write the word in the sentence.

empire (EM-pyr)

ruler (ROO-lur)

conqueror (KAHN-kur-ur)

1. A group of many countries controlled by one powerful leader is called an _____ .

2. A powerful leader, such a king or queen, is called a _____

3. Someone who fights and wins control over a country is called a _____ .

LEARN A SKILL: Using Maps

Where am I? Where did it happen? How can I get from place to place? How far away is it? Maps can help answer these and many other questions.

A **map** is a drawing of a real place. The first thing to look for when using a map is the title. The title will tell you what is being shown on the map.

Look at the map on page 13. Write the title.

_____

Every map has a direction arrow. It tells you that north (N) is toward the top of the map. South (S) is toward the bottom. West (W) is toward the left side, and east (E) is toward the right.

Find the direction arrow on the map on page 13. Copy it here.

MAKE PREDICTIONS

Read the title and headings. Use them to make predictions.

Put a (✔) mark next to the things you think you will learn about.

_____ who reached southern lands

_____ why the Mayan empire grew weak

_____ why the Aztec empire was strong

_____ who found the Aztec empire

_____ what lands Columbus found

_____ who claimed the Inca empire

Explorers Reach Southern Lands

1. Remember that conquistadores from Spain were exploring North America. At the same time, other explorers reached South America and Central America. (Find Central America between North and South America on the map on page 13.) These explorers also came to search for riches. They found valuable gold mines. They also found the great **empires** of the Mayas, Aztecs, and Incas. These empires were very large. The conquistadores hoped to claim these empires for Spain.

The Mayan Empire Grows Weak

2. The Mayan empire was in Mexico and Central America. The Mayan people had been living in these lands for hundreds of years. They built many beautiful cities, stone palaces, and huge pyramids. About 40,000 Mayan people lived in a city called Tikal.

LOOK

Look at the map on this page. Point to Tikal, which is in the Mayan empire.

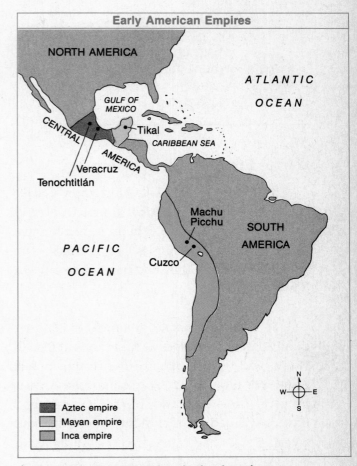

Early American Empires

NORTH AMERICA

ATLANTIC OCEAN

GULF OF MEXICO

CENTRAL AMERICA

Tikal

CARIBBEAN SEA

Veracruz

Tenochtitlán

Machu Picchu

SOUTH AMERICA

PACIFIC OCEAN

Cuzco

Aztec empire
Mayan empire
Inca empire

▲ This map shows empires in the Americas. Test yourself: Which empire is in South America?

3. During the late 800s, the Mayan empire became weak. Mayan cities fought each other. Many strong **rulers** were killed. The Mayans no longer had a strong leader.

4. Pedro de Alvarado (deh ahl-vah-RAH-doh) wanted to conquer the Mayans. He brought troops from Spain to the Mayan lands in 1523. Because the Mayans were weak, the troops quickly took control. More troops arrived from Spain in the 1540s, led by

Francisco de Montejo (deh mon-TEH-hoh). They conquered more Mayans.

The Aztec Empire Is Strong

5. The Aztec empire was north of the Mayan empire. The Aztecs were a fierce, strong people. They had built a large city called Tenochtitlán (teh-noch-tee-TLAHN). This city had great buildings and pyramids.

6. The Aztecs were feared by their neighbors because they were **conquerors.**

They fought with spears and with bows and arrows. They took the gold, corn, and animals of the people they conquered. To please the gods of their religion, the Aztecs sometimes killed these people.

TALK What do you think will happen when the Spanish meet the Aztecs? Talk about it with your classmates.

Cortés Finds the Aztec Empire

7. In the year 1519, Hernando Cortés (kohr-tehs) sailed to Mexico. Cortés wanted to claim Mexico for Spain. He brought 700 men, many guns, and 18 horses. The Aztecs were surprised because they had never seen guns or horses before.

8. It was not hard for Cortés to conquer the Aztecs. The Aztecs at first thought Cortés was a god. They did not harm him. Also, Aztec enemies helped Cortés fight the Aztecs. Finally, the guns and horses Cortés had brought helped his men fight better. In about a year, Cortés had conquered the whole Aztec empire.

REVIEW Why was it easy for Cortés to conquer the Aztecs? Hint: Read paragraph 8.

9. In the year 1520, Cortés left Tenochtitlán. Pedro de Alvarado ruled in place of Cortés. Alvarado was cruel to the Aztecs. The angry Aztecs began to fight the conquistadores. The Aztecs' leader tried to stop the fighting. The Aztecs killed him. The fighting continued until Cortés returned. But the city of Tenochtitlán was destroyed.

Pizarro Claims the Inca Empire

10. Another empire, the Inca empire, was thousands of miles away in Peru in South America. (Find the Inca empire on the map on page 13.) The Incas built great cities in the mountains. They built roads and strong bridges that are still used today.

11. Francisco Pizarro (pee-SAHR-oh) discovered the Incas. He decided to claim the Inca empire for Spain. Pizarro kidnapped and then killed the Inca leader. By the 1540s, the Incas had been defeated. Now Spain's empire included the Mayan, Aztec, and Inca empires.

▲ This drawing shows Spanish troops using guns and special bows and arrows. Test yourself: What are the Aztecs using?

CHECK THE OBJECTIVE: **Write down in your notebook the names of the three empires found by Spanish explorers in Central America and South America.**

UNDERSTANDING WHAT YOU HAVE READ

Read each pair of sentences. Underline the sentence that is <u>true</u>.

1. Spanish conquerors explored Mexico and Peru.
   Spanish conquerors did not explore Mexico or Peru.

2. Three empires were claimed by the Spanish conquerors.
   One empire was claimed by the Spanish conquerors.

3. The strong Mayans stopped the Spanish conquerors.
   The Mayans were too weak to stop the Spanish conquerors.

4. Hernando Cortés conquered the Aztec empire.
   Hernando Cortés conquered the Inca empire.

5. The Inca people had an empire in Central America.
   The Inca people had an empire in South America.

Spotlight on People: Malinche

Because the Aztecs had conquered her own people, Malinche helped Cortés. Malinche, who was a Native American, knew how to speak with the Spanish. So, she could make plans with Cortés and the Aztecs' enemies. These plans would make the Aztecs lose their empire to Spain.

Malinche saved Cortés and his men from danger. She married one of the explorers and moved with him to Spain.

No one is sure why Malinche helped Cortés. She might have helped him because she hated the Aztecs. Perhaps Cortés treated her well. Some people think Malinche helped Cortés because she loved him.

▲ Malinche and Cortés meet with the Aztec ruler.

THE SPANISH COLONIES

LEARN NEW WORDS

Say each word. Write the word in the sentence

colony (KAHL-uh-nee)

1. When people come to a new land, they live in a _____ that is run by their old country.

slave (SLAYV)

2. A person forced to work without pay for someone else is a _____ .

mission (MIH-shun)

3. The place where Native Americans were taught how to be Christians was called the _____ .

LEARN A SKILL: Turning Headings into Questions

Writing a heading as a **question** can help you remember what you read. Follow these steps to write a question.

- Use: <u>Who</u>, <u>What</u>, <u>Where</u>, <u>When</u>, <u>Why</u>, and <u>How</u>.
- You may need to change the order of the words or change a word.
- You may need to add words such as these: <u>do</u>, <u>did</u>, <u>were</u>, <u>are</u>, or <u>was</u>.
- Write a question mark (?) at the end of the question.

Write each heading on pages 17 and 18 as a question.

1. _____

2. _____

3. _____

4. _____

MAKE PREDICTIONS

Read the title and headings. Use them to make predictions.

Put a (✔) mark next to the things you think you will learn about.

_____ where Spain's colonies were _____ what goods were sent to Spain

_____ Native Americans in the colonies _____ why the Church came

_____ English explorers in the colonies _____ who explored the Grand Canyon

OBJECTIVE: Read to find out how people lived in the Spanish colonies.

TIP: The title and headings will help you.

Spain's Colonies in the New World

1. In Lesson 3 you learned that explorers from Spain conquered the Mayans, Aztecs, and Incas. The Spanish continued to conquer more lands. By the year 1600, most of South America had been claimed for Spain. Spain's **colonies** reached from what is now the United States (U.S.) to the southern tip of South America. People who settled in these colonies were called **colonists**.

2. The king of Spain gave land to the colonists. These large pieces of land were called **encomiendas** (en-koh-mee-EN-dahs). People who owned the land were called **encomenderos** (en-koh-men-DEH-rohs). The encomenderos owned everything on the land, including the Native Americans living there.

Native Americans in the Colonies

3. Many encomenderos treated the Native Americans badly. Some made them pay money, or **taxes**, to live on the land. Others forced them to work as **slaves**. Some colonists felt slavery was wrong.

4. One man asked the Spanish king to stop slavery. This man's name was Bartolomé de las Casas (deh lahs KAH-sahs). He said the Spanish explorers should give back what they had taken from the New World. He wanted them to return everything to the Native Americans.

5. Think about that for minute! Give everything back? The Spanish king did not return anything to the Native Americans, but he did stop slavery.

TALK Do you think Spain should have given back everything it had taken from the New World? Why? Talk about it with a friend.

6. Some encomenderos began paying Native Americans a little for their work. But most Native Americans stayed very poor and were overworked. Sometimes, all the people in a town died from working too hard. Many Native Americans also died from diseases such as small pox, brought by the colonists from Europe.

Colonies Send Goods to Spain

7. What work did the Native Americans do for the colonists? One job was **mining**, or digging metals from the ground. Colonists had found silver in the mines. Spain wanted this silver very much. So Native Americans

▲ Native Americans worked in this silver mine in the New World.

mined it for the encomenderos. Then groups of ships, called **treasure fleets**, carried the silver to Spain.

 Look at the map on page 3. Trace with your finger the route that treasure ships would have used to bring silver to Spain.

8. The Native Americans also grew crops on the encomenderos' farms. Some of the crops were new to the Americas. The colonists brought oranges, lemons, apples, rice, and sugar cane to the New World. Other crops were new to the colonists. The Native Americans grew potatoes, corn, peanuts, and tomatoes. The encomenderos had never tasted these foods before.

The Church Comes to the New World

9. The Catholic Church was an important part of life in the New World. The Church wanted to teach Native American people to be Christians. To do this, the Church started **missions**. Missions were part school, church, farm, and work place. **Priests** lived at the missions and worked as missionaries for the Church. They wanted Native Americans to come to the missions to learn how to become Christians.

 Why did the Catholic Church start missions? Hint: Read paragraph 9.

10. How did the Church get Native Americans to come to the missions? Priests gave them food, clothes, and a place to live. The Native Americans learned to read, write, and speak Spanish at the missions. At the same time, they learned about the Catholic Church. In return, Native Americans worked for the priests in the mission.

11. Some Native Americans got used to living on missions. Others thought mission life was like slavery. But over the years many Native Americans became Christians.

▲ The Spanish built great cities in the New World. Mexico City was built by the Spanish on top of the ruins of Tenochtitlán. (You learned in Lesson 3 that Tenochtitlán was built by the Aztecs.)

CHECK THE OBJECTIVE: Write down in your notebook one way people lived in the Spanish colonies.

AFTER YOU READ

Lesson 4

UNDERSTANDING WHAT YOU HAVE READ

Read the words in the box. Then write a word on each line.

colonists	Native Americans	Christians
missions	corn	silver

1. People living in the Spanish colonies were called _____ .

2. One of the most important goods sent back to Spain was _____ .

3. Priests wanted to teach Native Americans to be _____ .

4. Some of the encomenderos used _____ as slaves.

5. Native Americans taught the Spanish how to grow _____ .

6. The Spanish built _____ where they taught Native Americans about the Christian religion.

Spotlight on People: Bartolomé de las Casas

Bartolomé de las Casas came to the New World in the year 1502. He was both an encomendero and a Catholic priest. At first, las Casas used Native American slaves to work on his encomienda. Then he changed his mind. He saw that slavery was killing the Native Americans. He told the king of Spain his ideas. He asked the king to free the slaves. He also wanted Spain to return everything it had taken from the New World.

Colonists did not want las Casas to tell them what to do. They forced him to move away from the colonies. Las Casas kept fighting for the Native Americans. He wrote books about the way the colonists treated them. He is remembered today as the priest who cared about the Native Americans.

▲ Bartolomé de las Casas wrote a letter to the Spanish king.

REVIEW 1

SUMMARY OF LESSONS 1-4

Here are some important ideas you learned in Lessons 1-4. Write the one you want to remember.

- Christopher Columbus sailed from Spain to the New World in 1492. (1)

- Many Spanish explorers came to search for riches in the New World. (2)

- Spanish explorers in Central America and South America conquered the Mayans, Aztecs, and Incas. (3)

- Spanish settlers brought many new foods, such as oranges, apples, rice, and sugar cane to the New World. (4)

- Native Americans worked on farms and in mines for the encomenderos. (4)

- The Catholic Church started missions to teach the Christian religion to Native Americans. (4)

REVIEWING NEW WORDS

Look up the words below in the Glossary. Write the correct word in each sentence.

coast (2)	colony (4)	island (1)
government (4)	empire (3)	route (1)

1. The Inca _____ was in Peru in South America.

2. Columbus was looking for a shorter _____ to Asia.

3. An _____ is land with water on all sides.

4. The encomendero lived in a Spanish _____ in California.

5. The _____ is the area of land along the ocean.

6. In Mexico City, a small group of colonists ran the _____ .

REVIEWING WHAT YOU HAVE READ

Find the correct answer to each question. Circle the letter.

1. Queen Isabella helped Columbus by
   a. saying his plan would not work.
   b. giving him money to buy ships.
   c. asking the Church to give him money.

2. After Columbus discovered the New World, it was
   a. explored by many conquistadores.
   b. forgotten for many years.
   c. visited only by a few missionaries.

3. In Mexico, Hernando Cortés conquered
   a. the Inca empire.
   b. the Mayan empire.
   c. the Aztec empire.

4. Silver was carried from the colonies to Spain
   a. in treasure fleets.
   b. by horses.
   c. in one large boat.

REVIEWING SKILLS

Study the map. Then answer the questions.

1. Which explorers sailed north along the Pacific coast? _____

_____

2. Which explorer crossed the Mississippi River? _____

3. Who sailed along the Florida coast? _____

_____

4. Which explorer traveled farthest north on land? _____

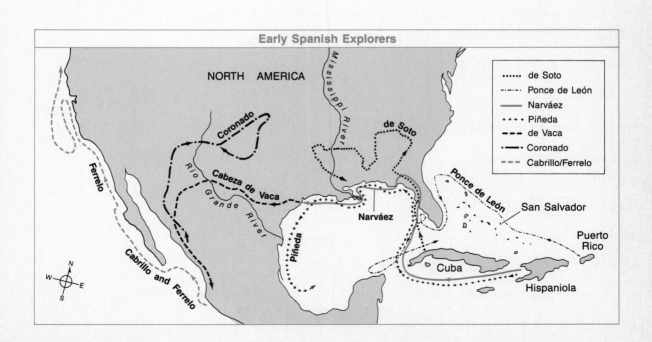

Early Spanish Explorers

SETTLEMENT OF FLORIDA

LEARN NEW WORDS

Say each word. Write the word in the sentence.

settlement (SET-ul-munt)

1. A new town that a group of people start is called a
_____ .

permanent (PUR-muh-nunt)

2. Something that does not disappear or change, but continues to last, is called _____ .

soldiers (SOL-jurs)

3. People who fight to protect their country are called
_____ .

LEARN A SKILL: Finding the Main Idea

The important ideas in readings are called **main ideas**. Look for main ideas in:

- headings
- sentences

A main idea sentence tells about all the other sentences in a paragraph. The main idea may be in the first sentence, the middle sentence, or the last sentence in a paragraph.

Read paragraph 7 on page 24. Find the sentence that is the main idea of the paragraph. Remember, it tells about all the other sentences.

Write the main idea sentence.

_____

In this paragraph the main idea sentence is

_____ the first sentence.   _____ in the middle.   _____ the last sentence.

MAKE PREDICTIONS

Read the title and headings. Use them to make predictions.

Put a (✔) next to the things you think you will learn about.

_____ why Spain needed Florida   _____ how big Florida is today

_____ where the first settlement was   _____ the Spanish in Mexico

_____ where other settlements were   _____ when St. Augustine was started

OBJECTIVE: **Read to find out why the Spanish wanted to settle in Florida.**

TIP: **Finding the main ideas will help you.**

Spain Needs Florida

1. Spain claimed the area that is now called Florida, in the year 1513. Because Florida had no gold or silver, no **settlements** had been started there.

2. Then Spain found a good reason to settle Florida. Remember the treasure fleets? These ships carried riches from the New World back to Spain. But French, Dutch, and British ships would attack the fleets. The Spanish decided that settlements in Florida could protect the treasure fleets.

First Settlement Is Started

3. In 1526, Lucas Vázquez de Ayllón (deh ah-YOHN) tried to settle in Florida. The king of Spain had named Ayllón **adelantado** (ah-deh-lahn-TAH-doh), or governor, of Florida. Ayllón set sail from Hispaniola with 600 people and 89 horses. But strong winds blew the ships too far north. The ships landed in what is now South Carolina. The people started a settlement there called San Miguel de Gualdape (sahn mee-GEHL deh gwal-DAH-peh).

4. Ayllón and his people were **settlers**. This means they were the first to come to live in a new place. The settlers with Ayllón began to build. They built homes, a church, and a place to store their supplies.

5. But problems arose because of the cold winter that year. Many people became sick.

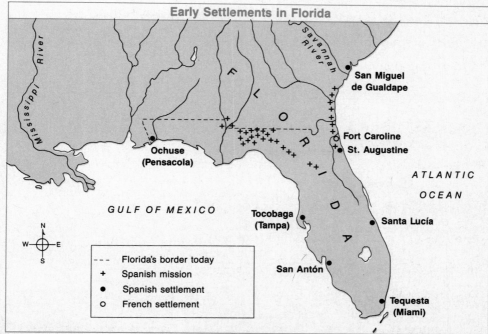

▲ This map shows early settlements in Florida. Test yourself: What French settlement is shown on the map?

Over 400 settlers died from sickness and hunger. Ayllón also died. Early in the year 1527, the rest of the settlers returned to Hispaniola. San Miguel de Gualdape was not a permanent settlement. But it was the first European settlement in what is now the United States.

Other Settlements Are Started

6. In 1559, another settlement was started. A man named Tristán de Luna y Arellano (deh LOO-nah ee ah-rehl-YAH-noh) brought over 1,000 colonists to Ochuse (oh-CHYOOS). Five hundred **soldiers** also came along to protect the colonists. De Luna brought 240 horses, too.

LOOK Look at the map on page 23. Find Ochuse on the map. What city now stands where Ochuse was built?

---

7. The colonists with de Luna faced many problems. A storm destroyed their ships. The people lost tools and other supplies. After some time, the colonists began to starve. De Luna tried to start another settlement away from the coast. Neither of these settlements became permanent.

St. Augustine Becomes Permanent

8. Meanwhile, the Spanish king was worried about French settlers. They had built a settlement in Florida called Fort Caroline. The king did not want a French colony in Spain's empire. He ordered Pedro Menéndez de Avilés (meh-NEN-dehs deh ah-vee-LEHS) to build a permanent settlement in Florida. The king ordered Menéndez to force the French settlers out.

9. In 1565, Menéndez began a settlement called St. Augustine. His men built a **fort**. A fort is where soldiers live. It is built strong to keep enemies out. Spanish soldiers attacked the French colony. Most of the French people were killed. Menéndez brought more people to live in St. Augustine. He also started other settlements in Florida.

10. St. Augustine was the first permanent settlement in Florida. By the late 1600s, more than 1,000 people lived there. St. Augustine is the oldest city in the U.S.

▲ Castillo de San Marcos is the oldest fort in the United States. The fort was built in St. Augustine.

CHECK THE OBJECTIVE: **Write down in your notebook one reason the Spanish wanted to settle in Florida.**

UNDERSTANDING WHAT YOU HAVE READ

Find the correct answer to each question. Circle the letter.

1. Why did Spain need Florida?
   a. to mine gold from the land
   b. to help protect the treasure fleets
   c. to conquer the Native Americans

2. Where was the first European settlement in the U.S.?
   a. South Carolina
   b. Texas
   c. Spain

3. What made life difficult for the early settlers?
   a. bad weather, sickness, little food
   b. not enough money
   c. high taxes

4. What was a permanent settlement?
   a. one that disappeared
   b. one with many sick people
   c. one that lasted

5. What happened to the early French settlers in Florida?
   a. The Spanish welcomed them.
   b. The Spanish forced them out.
   c. They conquered La Florida.

6. What was the name of the first permanent settlement in Florida?
   a. Pensacola
   b. Ochuse
   c. St. Augustine

Arts and Technology: Castillo de San Marcos

In 1672, workers began building a fort at St. Augustine, Florida. The fort was named Castillo de San Marcos (kah-STEE-yoh deh san-MAR-kohs).

The fort was special because it was made of stone. All of the earlier forts at St. Augustine had been made of wood. A stone fort would be stronger than a wooden fort.

After many years, the fort was finished. Inside the fort were a chapel and a place for soldiers to live. The fort also had places to keep food, guns, and other goods. All around the fort there was a wide ditch filled with water. The ditch helped to keep enemies out of the fort.

▲ An artist drew this picture of St. Augustine, Florida about 100 years after it was settled. You can see Castillo de San Marcos on the far side of the river. Compare this picture with the drawing of the fort on page 24.

NEW MEXICO AND ARIZONA

LEARN NEW WORDS

Say each word. Write the word in the sentence.

convert (kun-VURT)

1. To change a person's beliefs or religion is to _____ that person.

founded (FOWND-ed)

2. A place that is set up or started, such as a new city, is _____ .

rebellion (rih-BEL-yun)

3. A fight against rulers or a government is a _____ .

LEARN A SKILL: Finding Details

You remember that the first sentence in a paragraph often gives the main idea of the paragraph. But what do the other sentences do? Think of the main idea as a big umbrella. The other sentences are like the spokes of the umbrella. They hold it up. They tell more about the main idea. They are called **details**. Details answer the questions <u>Who</u>? <u>What</u>? <u>Why</u>? <u>When</u>? and <u>How</u>?

Read paragraph 2 on page 27. The main idea sentence is "Oñate was governor of New Mexico from the year 1598 to 1607."

Now write the detail sentences:

_____

_____

_____

_____

MAKE PREDICTIONS

Read the title and headings. Use them to make predictions.

Put a (✔) mark next to the things you think you will learn about.

_____ when settlers came from Mexico   _____ why Native Americans rebelled

_____ important Mexican crops   _____ who rules Mexico today

_____ who governed New Mexico   _____ when the Spanish settled Arizona

OBJECTIVE: Read to find out which Spanish leaders settled New Mexico and Arizona.

TIP: The main idea and details will help you.

WHILE YOU READ

Lesson 6

Settlers Come From Mexico

1. Remember the "Seven Cities of Gold"? Coronado looked for them in the Southwest in 1540. Many years later, an explorer started the first Spanish settlement in New Mexico. This explorer was Juan de Oñate (deh oh-NYEH-teh). He led people north from Mexico in 1598. They began a settlement called San Juan de Los Caballeros (san wahn deh lohs kah-bah-YER-ohs). Missionaries came with the settlers. They began to **convert** Native Americans to the Christian religion.

 REREAD Where did the people come from who started the first settlement in New Mexico?

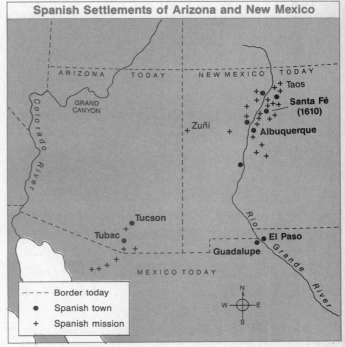

Spanish Settlements of Arizona and New Mexico

- - - - Border today
● Spanish town
+ Spanish mission

▲ This map shows early Spanish towns and missions. Test yourself: Was Zuni started as a town or a mission? as a mission

2. Oñate was governor of New Mexico from the year 1598 to 1607. Even as governor, he kept exploring. He looked for gold. He also looked for a waterway to the Pacific Ocean. Then Oñate went back to New Mexico. His enemies said he treated the Native Americans badly. In 1607, Oñate resigned as governor.

New Mexico Gets a New Governor

3. Pedro de Peralta (deh per-AHL-tuh) became the new governor of New Mexico. The Spanish king ordered him to start a capital for New Mexico. In 1610, Peralta **founded** the city of Santa Fe. Santa Fe is the oldest state capital in the U.S. today.

4. Peralta had Native Americans build a **government** center. This building is the oldest government building in the U.S. The building is made of **adobe** (ah-DOH-beh). Adobe is mud and straw dried in the sun. Native

Americans in New Mexico and Arizona had built with adobe for many years.

5. Peralta, along with people who owned property, ran the government. These people elected the members of the **cabildo** (kah-BEEL-doh), or town council. Problems soon started between the government and the Catholic Church. Each group thought the other group treated the Native Americans badly.

Native Americans Rebel

6. It is true that the Native Americans were very unhappy living under Spanish rule. The colonists made the Native Americans work very hard. They made them pay **tribute**

to the Spanish. A tribute was a kind of tax that was paid in corn, cloth, or by work. The Spanish did not let the Native Americans own horses. The Spanish forced the Native Americans to convert to be Christians.

 REVIEW How did the Native Americans feel living under Spanish rule?

7. Imagine being a Native American at that time. What would you have done? In 1676, the first Native American **rebellion** against the Spanish was started by the Apaches. In 1680, a Native American named Pope (poh-PAY) started another rebellion. Pope led Native Americans living in many different towns, or **pueblos** (pweh-blohs), in this rebellion. Most of the Spanish settlers were killed. Some Native Americans who had been converted to Christianity gave up the religion. Most of the Spanish settlements in New Mexico were destroyed. Would the Spanish ever rule over New Mexico again?

 TALK Imagine you are a Spanish settler in New Mexico. Native Americans killed many of your neighbors. Would you stay in New Mexico or leave? Why?

8. Twelve years later, a new Spanish governor came to New Mexico. His name was Diego de Vargas (deh VAR-gahs). Vargas had to conquer the Native Americans in New Mexico all over again. By the year 1696, Spain ruled New Mexico again.

The Spanish Settle Arizona

9. The Spanish settled Arizona much later than New Mexico. An explorer found silver in Arizona in the 1580s. But the silver was hard to reach and to mine. In the 1690s, a missionary set up missions in Arizona to convert the Native Americans there.

10. In 1821, Mexico won its independence from Spain. Then Mexico ruled over New Mexico and Arizona until 1848.

▲Many Native Americans in New Mexico and Arizona lived in pueblos. A pueblo is like a small town. This is the Taos Pueblo in New Mexico.

CHECK THE OBJECTIVE: **Write a sentence in your notebook telling about one Spanish leader who settled New Mexico.**

UNDERSTANDING WHAT YOU HAVE READ

Read each pair of sentences. Underline the sentence that is <u>true</u>.

1. The early settlers in New Mexico came from Florida.
   The early settlers in New Mexico came from Mexico.

2. Oñate resigned as governor of New Mexico.
   Oñate was the only governor of New Mexico for many, many years.

3. Santa Fe was founded by Peralto, a governor of New Mexico.
   Santa Fe was founded by the French.

4. Native Americans started a rebellion against the Spanish.
   Native Americans never started a rebellion against the Spanish.

5. The Spanish settled Arizona before they settled New Mexico.
   The Spanish settled Arizona after they settled New Mexico.

6. Mexico won its independence from Spain in the year 1821.
   Mexico lost its independence to Spain in the year 1821.

Spotlight on People: Diego de Vargas

Diego de Vargas was born in Spain. He came from a wealthy family. He became governor of New Mexico in 1691. At that time, the land was controlled by Native Americans. Most Spanish settlers had been killed during the Native American rebellion. The remaining settlers were very poor and hungry. They did not have enough food or supplies. They wanted to move to Mexico.

Vargas would not let the Spanish settlers leave New Mexico. He wanted to take control of New Mexico and the Native Americans. With very little fighting, he conquered 77 pueblos. Then he went to Mexico to bring back more Spanish settlers. By 1696, New Mexico was once again under Spanish rule.

▲ Diego de Vargas won control of New Mexico from the Native Americans.

SETTLEMENT OF TEXAS

LEARN NEW WORDS

Say each word. Write the word in the sentence.

invade (in-VAYD)

1. When you enter a country in order to attack it, you _____ the country.

ruins (ROO-uns)

2. When something is destroyed, what is left is called the _____ .

independence (in-duh-PEN-duns)

3. When you are free from the rule of others, you have your _____ .

LEARN A SKILL: Using Different Kinds of Maps

A **picture map** has pictures on it that show where to find things.

Find the picture map on page 32. Write the title.

_____

Now find the map key. The key is on the right side.

Write the letter to match each picture with the words on the key that tell about it.

_____ 1.   _____ 3.

a. waterways

b. missions

c. buildings for hidalgos

_____ 2.   _____ 4.

d. farms

MAKE PREDICTIONS

Read the title and headings. Use them to make predictions.

Put a (✔) mark next to the things you think you will learn about.

_____ why the Spanish settled Texas   _____ what problems the missions had

_____ when the French came to Texas   _____ why the U.S. and Mexico fought

_____ who built forts in Texas   _____ how Texas became part of Mexico

OBJECTIVE: Read to find out why Spanish people settled in Texas.

TIP: The title and headings will help you.

WHILE YOU READ

Lesson 7

Spanish Settlements in Texas

1. By 1680, Spain ruled many lands in the New World. It ruled Mexico and much of South America. The Spanish had settled Florida, Arizona, and New Mexico. But what about Texas? Spanish explorers were in Texas in the 1500s. Had any Spanish settled there?

2. In 1680, there were no Spanish settlements in Texas. Spanish explorers did not find gold in Texas so they did not claim it. Spanish rulers in Europe needed money. They wanted their colonists in the New World to find riches. Because Texas had no gold, it was not included in the Spanish empire.

 REREAD Why were there no Spanish settlements in Texas?

3. Sometimes people do not want something until others want it. This is what happened with Texas. Spain discovered that another country was interested in Texas.

The French Come to Texas

4. In 1682, the French came to Texas. The French explorer La Salle (lah SAL) sailed down the Mississippi River. He called the area around the Mississippi "Louisiana." La Salle claimed Louisiana for France. He reached the Texas coast on the Gulf of Mexico. Then he built a fort and called it Fort St. Louis. La Salle hoped to **invade** and conquer part of Mexico.

5. Spanish rulers did not want France to have Texas. They did not want France to conquer a part of Mexico either. The Spanish

▲ Native Americans dig a ditch at a Spanish mission in Texas.

sent Captain Alonso de León to Fort St. Louis, to force the French out of Texas.

6. When de León got to Fort St. Louis, he found no French people. The fort was empty and in ruins. Native Americans had invaded the fort and killed all the French. All that was left of Fort St. Louis was ruins.

Early Missions and Forts in Texas

7. Spain decided it was time to build Spanish settlements in Texas. In 1690, Captain de León went back to eastern Texas with a missionary. This missionary set up the first mission in eastern Texas.

8. The Spanish built many more missions in eastern and central Texas. They also built forts, or **presidios** (preh-SEE-dyohs). The modern city of San Antonio, in central Texas, began as a mission and a fort.

Problems in the Missions

9. The Spanish missions in Texas had problems. One problem was growing enough food for the settlers. Some of the settlers had the title of **hidalgo** (ee-DAHL-goh), or gentleman, in Spain. Other people had done the work for the hidalgos in Spain. Hidalgos would not work with their hands. They would not farm. So the missions had trouble growing enough food for everyone.

 Look at the picture map of San Antonio. Point to the presidio. Hint: Use the map key.

10. The Spanish missions had another big problem. Native Americans attacked Spanish missions. The Apaches were the Native Americans who attacked most often.

11. How could settlers be safe from the Apaches? A leader was sent by the king of Spain. He said all the settlers should move to San Antonio and another large mission. Then the Spanish soldiers could protect the settlers from the Apaches. The Spanish leader thought the settlers should fight the Apaches.

12. Some settlers from eastern Texas moved to San Antonio, as they were told. They got new land there, but the settlers were not happy. Their new land was not very good for farming. They asked the leader if they could move back to eastern Texas. The settlers were allowed to go back to their land.

Texas Becomes Part of Mexico

13. In the year 1821, Mexico won its **independence** from Spain. This meant that Mexico became a new country, free from Spanish rule. Texas was part of the land of Mexico. So Texas became part of the new country of Mexico.

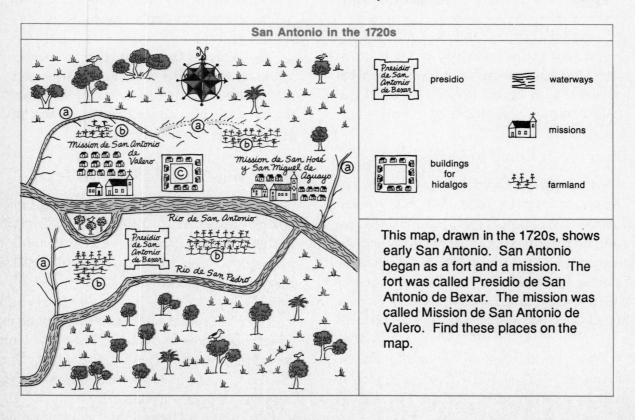

San Antonio in the 1720s

Presidio de San Antonio de Bexar — presidio
waterways
buildings for hidalgos
missions
farmland

This map, drawn in the 1720s, shows early San Antonio. San Antonio began as a fort and a mission. The fort was called Presidio de San Antonio de Bexar. The mission was called Mission de San Antonio de Valero. Find these places on the map.

CHECK THE OBJECTIVE: **Write down in your notebook one reason Spanish people decided to settle in Texas.**

UNDERSTANDING WHAT YOU HAVE READ

Read each pair of sentences. Underline the sentence that is <u>true</u>.

1. The Spanish settled in Texas in the 1800s.
    The Spanish settled in Texas in the 1600s.

2. Texas had no silver or gold mines.
    Texas had many silver and gold mines.

3. La Salle was a French explorer who built Fort St. Louis.
    La Salle was a French explorer who invaded Mexico.

4. The modern city of San Antonio began as a mission and fort.
    No missions were built near what is now San Antonio.

5. Texas became part of Mexico.
    Texas never became part of Mexico.

Spotlight on People: Antonio Gil Ybarbo

Antonio Gil Ybarbo (ee-BAR-boh) lived in eastern Texas with other Spanish settlers. They moved into the woods and farmed the land. They raised animals. They got along well with the Native Americans.

One day, a Spanish leader, sent by the king, ordered the settlers to leave eastern Texas. He ordered them to San Antonio to be safe from Apaches. Ybarbo and his friends did not want to leave. They felt San Antonio was dangerous because the Apaches often attacked it. But the Spanish leader made them come to San Antonio.

Ybarbo's group was unhappy in San Antonio. All the best land had been taken. They asked the ruler to let them go back home. The ruler said they could.

Ybarbo and his neighbors moved back to eastern Texas. They built a fort. Ybarbo became the leader of this settlement, called Nacogdoches (nah-kuh-DOH-ches). Descendants of Ybarbo and his group still live in Nacogdoches today.

▲Ybarbo and other settlers come to Nacogdoches.

SETTLEMENT OF CALIFORNIA

LEARN NEW WORDS

Say each word. Write the word in the sentence.

nations (NAY-shuns)

region (REE-jun)

peninsula (puh-NIN-suh-luh)

1. The world has many countries or _____ .

2. A large area of land is called a _____ .

3. A piece of land with water on three sides is a

   _____ .

LEARN A SKILL: Using Key Words

A **key word** names a special person, place, or thing. A capital letter is the sign for a key word. Look at these words: **Native American**.

Do you know whether these words name a person, place, or thing? Let's say you do not know. To find out, read the other words in the sentence. The other words will tell you. Read this sentence: What crops did the **Native American** grow?

Can a thing grow a crop? Can a place grow a crop? This sentence tells you that the key words **Native American** name a person.

Read the sentences. Write person, place, or thing for each key word. Use the other words in the sentence to help you.

> **Hint:**
>
> Look for capital letters at the middle or end of a sentence.

1. They built settlements in **Upper California**.
   Upper California names a _____ .

2. People in Europe controlled the **Catholic Church**.
   Catholic Church names a _____ .

3. The explorer was **Gaspar de Portolá**.
   Gaspar de Portolá names a _____ .

MAKE PREDICTIONS

Read the title and headings. Use them to make predictions.

Put a (✔) mark next to the things you think you will learn about.

_____ how Spain protected its land

_____ why California was settled

_____ how to move to California

_____ how Mexico won independence

_____ which rulers had the most money

_____ how life was on Mexican ranchos

OBJECTIVE: Read to find about types of early Spanish settlements in California.

TIP: Understanding key words can help you.

Spain Wants to Protect its Land

1. The Spanish king had problems. Other **nations** wanted to take over Spain's land in the New World. The French had already tried to settle in Texas and Florida. Now Russian traders were moving south toward California. They were coming down along the Pacific coast. How could the king protect Spain's land in California? He decided to begin settlements there.

2. California was a large **region** of land with two parts. One part was called Baja (BAH-hah) California. The word <u>baja</u> means "lower" in Spanish. Baja California is a **peninsula** off the coast of Mexico. Some Spanish settlers already lived on this peninsula. The Spanish called the northern part of the region Upper California. Today, Upper California is the state of California.

LOOK Look at the map on this page. Part of the peninsula of Baja California is shown. Point to it.

Settlements in California Begin

3. To keep other nations from claiming its land, Spain began to settle Upper California. The government sent Gaspar de Portolá (deh por-toh-LAH) to start settlements. In 1769, Portolá set up the first presidio. A missionary named Father Junípero Serra (SER-rah) went to set up missions. In 1769, Father Serra set up the first mission in the region. By the 1820s, there were 21 missions in Upper California.

4. The Spanish planned three kinds of settlements in California. These were missions, presidios, and pueblos. Remember, you learned in Lesson 6 that Native Americans built pueblos in New Mexico and Arizona. Spanish colonists would also live in pueblos in California. (Look back at page 28 for a picture of a pueblo.)

REREAD What three kinds of settlements did the Spanish plan to build in California?

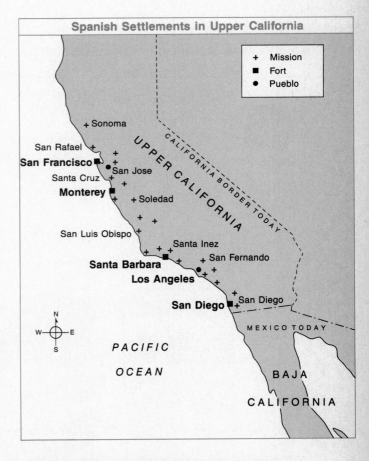

▲ The map shows Spanish settlements in Upper California. Test yourself: How many presidios, or forts, are shown on the map?
Four presidios are shown on the map.

Mexico Wins Independence

5. In 1821, Mexico won its independence from Spain. Now California, along with Texas, was a part of the nation of Mexico. The new Mexican government passed a law called the **Secularization** (sek-yoo-luh-ruh-ZAY-shun) **Act**. What does <u>secularization</u> mean? Secularization means changing something from religious, or church, control to nonreligious, or government, control.

6. Mexico's Secularization Act changed the way California missions were run. Before this law, mission land was controlled by the Church. After this law, mission land was no longer controlled by the Church. Some of the land was sold to settlers. The rest was given to Native Americans. But most Native Americans soon lost control over their land.

 How did a new law affect California missions? Hint: The third sentence in paragraph 6 will help you.

Life on the Mexican Ranchos

7. The Mexican government sold and gave away large areas of land called **ranchos** (RAHN-chos). By the 1840s, there were more than 800 ranchos in California. The owners, or **rancheros** (rahn-CHEH-rohs), raised cattle for the skins, or hides. These hides were made into leather for clothes, boots, and other things. Rancheros also sold animal fat, or tallow, from the cattle. People used tallow to make candles and soap. The rancheros hired cowboys, called **vaqueros** (vah-KEH-rohs), to take care of the cattle.

 Would you have liked being a vaquero? What do you think would be hard about the job? Talk about it with your classmates.

8. The ranchos were the center of life in Mexican California. Other settlers came to live in California. Some of them started ranchos of their own.

▲ The Santa Barbara Mission was begun in the year 1786. This building was built in 1815. Like many missions, the Santa Barbara Mission was named for a saint. <u>Santa</u> means "saint" in Spanish. The Santa Barbara Mission was named for the saint who was said to keep sailors safe.

CHECK THE OBJECTIVE: Write down in your notebook one type of early the Spanish settlement in California.

UNDERSTANDING WHAT YOU HAVE READ

Find the correct answer to each question. Circle the letter.

1. How did Spain protect its claims in California?
   a. Spain sent Russian traders to guard the land.
   b. Spain's army fought a war.
   c. Spain started Spanish settlements.

2. What is the lower part of California called?
   a. Upper California
   b. Baja California
   c. Middle California

3. What happened to California when Mexico became an independent nation?
   a. California became part of Canada.
   b. California became part of Mexico.
   c. All Spanish settlers left California.

4. Why did most rancheros raise cattle?
   a. It was a Spanish law.
   b. Rancheros raised cattle for their hides and tallow.
   c. Only cattle could live in California.

Spotlight on People: Father Junípero Serra

Father Junípero Serra was a missionary who helped Spain settle Upper California. Father Serra went to Mexico in 1749. He worked as a missionary there. Then he went to Upper California to set up missions. He led a group of 17 missionaries. Father Serra's group traveled with Gaspar de Portolá, who was sent by Spain to start settlements.

The trip to Upper California was hard for Father Serra because he had trouble walking. But Father Serra believed strongly that he should convert the Native Americans to be Christians. The first mission he built was in San Diego. Father Serra built eight more missions. After Father Serra died in 1784, other people built more missions. By the 1820s, Upper California had 21 missions.

▲ Father Junípero Serra was a missionary in California. A statue honoring Father Serra is in the U.S. Capitol building in Washington, D.C.

REVIEW 2

SUMMARY OF LESSONS 5-8

Here are some important ideas you learned in Lessons 5-8. Write the one you want to remember.

- The first permanent Spanish settlement in Florida was St. Augustine. (5)

- Juan de Oñate started the first Spanish settlement in New Mexico and became its governor. (6)

- Native Americans attacked Spanish missions in Texas. (7)

- The Spanish built missions, presidios, and pueblos in California. (8)

- Life for many settlers in California changed when they became rancheros. (8)

REVIEWING NEW WORDS

Look up the words below in the Glossary. Write the correct word in each sentence.

settlement (5)	founded(6)	independence (7)
rebellion (6)	peninsula (8)	region (8)

1. In 1821, Mexico won its _____ from Spain.

2. A _____ is a fight against rulers or a government.

3. Baja California is a _____ off the coast of Mexico.

4. San Miguel de Gualdape was the first European _____ in America.

5. A _____ is a large area of land.

6. The city of Santa Fe was _____ in 1610.

REVIEWING WHAT YOU HAVE READ

Write **T** if a sentence is true. Write **F** is the sentence is false.

_____ 1. Spain built settlements in Florida to help protect its treasure fleets.

_____ 2. Native Americans used wood to build the oldest government building in the U.S.

_____ 3. Arizona was settled before New Mexico.

_____ 4. The French built a fort in Texas before the Spanish settled there.

_____ 5. Spanish missions in Texas had trouble growing enough food for the settlers.

_____ 6. Mexico passed the Secularization Act, which gave land to the Catholic Church.

REVIEWING SKILLS

Study the map. Then answer the questions.

Circle the letter of the correct answer.

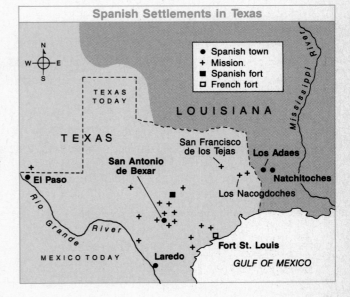

1. Which part of Texas had the most missions?
   a. west
   b. central
   c. east

2. San Antonio de Bexar became the modern city of
   a. San Antonio
   b. San Francisco
   c. St. Louis

3. Fort St. Louis was built near the
   a. Gulf of Mexico
   b. Mississippi River
   c. Texas border

4. How many Spanish towns were in French Louisiana?
   a. 1
   b. 2
   c. 3

SPAIN AND LOUISIANA

LEARN NEW WORDS

Say each word. Write the word in the sentence.

territory (TER-uh-tor-ee)

official (uh-FISH-ul)

duties (DOOT-eez)

1. A large area of land held by a ruler or a nation is called a
_____ .

2. Something that is done according to rules or laws is said to be
_____ .

3. A government collects taxes, or _____ , on goods.

LEARN A SKILL: Using Time Lines

When did it happen? Before or after something else happened? How long ago did it happen? Thinking about time when you read will help you understand history better.

To find out when things happened, look for dates in the reading. Look for **time lines**. A time line is a bar, or thick line. It has years or periods of time marked on the line to show the order in which things happened.

> **Hint:**
> Look for years in order on a time line.

There are other ways to find out about the time of events when reading. Look for words that order time, such as <u>first</u>, <u>next</u>, <u>then</u>, <u>after</u>, <u>later</u>, and <u>during</u>. Look for dates such as months, years, and seasons.

Find the time line on page 42. Write the title.

_____

How many years are shown on the time line?

_____

MAKE PREDICTIONS

Read the title and headings. Use them to make predictions.

Put a (✔) mark next to the things you think you will learn about.

_____ who gave Louisiana to Spain

_____ why settlers rebelled

_____ how forts were built

_____ why Louisiana prospered

_____ how Spain lost Louisiana

_____ how Louisiana's climate was

OBJECTIVE: **Read to find out who gave Louisiana to Spain.**

TIP: **The title and headings will help you.**

Louisiana Is Given to Spain

1. Spain was not the only nation with land in the New World. Spain ruled over land in Florida, the Southwest, and California. What about the land between Florida and the Southwest? France and Great Britain both claimed parts of this region.

2. In the middle of the 1700s, France and Great Britain fought over their **territories** in the New World. Spain helped France in the war against the British. Because of this, France secretly gave Louisiana to Spain. France later lost the war to Great Britain. But Spain kept Louisiana and became its **official** ruler in 1763.

 LOOK Find Spanish Louisiana on the map on this page. Was this territory bigger than the state of Louisiana?

Settlers Start a Rebellion

3. Spain sent a governor to rule Louisiana. His name was Antonio de Ulloa (deh oo-LYOH-ah). The French settlers in Louisiana were unhappy with the new governor. He wanted the settlers to trade only with Spain. The settlers wanted to trade with other countries, too. The new governor also collected **duties**, or taxes, from the settlers. This made the settlers angry. They started a rebellion. They forced Ulloa to leave. The settlers then tried to set up their own government.

Louisiana in 1763

CANADA

GREAT LAKES

Mississippi River

LOUISIANA

St. Louis
Cahokia
Fort Charles
Kaskaskia
New Madrid

San Fernando
Arkansas
Nogales

TEXAS

Natchez
Baton Rouge
Manchac
New Orleans

GULF OF MEXICO

Land claimed by Spain
Land claimed by Great Britain
□ British fort
■ Spanish fort
- - - - Louisiana border today

▲ This map shows the Louisiana territory that was given to Spain. Test yourself: What river flowed between the British colonies and Louisiana?

 REVIEW Why were settlers in Louisiana angry with the Spanish governor? Hint: The fourth and sixth sentences in paragraph 3 will help you.

4. What do you think the Spanish king did when he heard about the rebellion? He sent **troops** to Louisiana. He put a man named Alexander O'Reilly in charge of the troops. O'Reilly was an Irishman who served in the Spanish army. He brought peace back to the territory.

Louisiana Grows and Prospers

5. Spain controlled Louisiana for about 30 years. Other Spanish governors ruled in Louisiana. One governor was Bernardo de Gálvez (deh GAHL-vehs). He invited settlers from other colonies in America and Canada to live in Louisiana.

6. Louisiana became a good place to live. Settlers in Louisiana began to grow and sell large crops of sugar cane. The people made money, and the Louisiana territory became wealthy.

 Which crop did Louisiana farmers grow?

Spain Loses Louisiana

7. Meanwhile, France had a new ruler. His name was Napoleon Bonaparte (BOH-nah-part). Remember in paragraph 2 you read that France had given Louisiana to Spain. Now Napoleon wanted Louisiana back. In the year 1800, Spain returned Louisiana to France.

8. Spain had ruled Louisiana for 40 years. In the meantime, the nation of the United States (U.S.) had been founded. The new nation went as far west as the Mississippi River. Farmers sent their crops on boats down the river to the Gulf of Mexico. But the **mouth** of the river was not part of the United States. It was in Louisiana, which belonged to France. Americans wanted to control the mouth of the Mississippi River.

9. American leaders offered to buy Louisiana from France. In 1803, Napoleon agreed. The United States bought the Louisiana territory. This was called the **Louisiana Purchase**. Americans controlled the mouth of the Mississippi River and the lands to the west. French rule and Spanish rule over Louisiana had ended.

 What if France had kept Louisiana? How do you think life would be different in the U.S. if Louisiana were under French rule now? Talk about it with a partner.

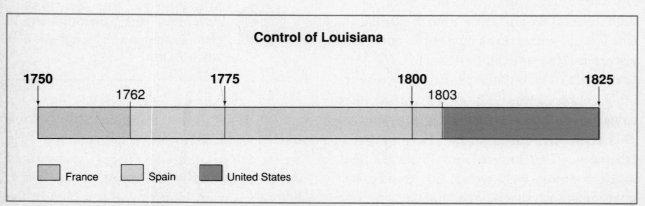

Control of Louisiana

1750   1762   1775   1800   1803   1825

France   Spain   United States

▲ This time line shows which nations ruled Louisiana from the years 1750 to 1825. Test yourself: France ruled the Louisiana territory from the years 1750 to 1762. Who took over control in the year 1762? Use the key under the time line to help you find the answer.

CHECK THE OBJECTIVE: Write a sentence in your notebook telling who gave Louisiana to Spain. How did Spain lose its rule over Louisiana?

UNDERSTANDING WHAT YOU HAVE READ

Read the words in the box. Write the word that completes each sentence.

mouth	sugar cane	territory
Spain	rebellion	Napoleon

1. France and Britain fought a war over _____ in the New World.

2. France gave Louisiana to _____ for helping them fight the war against Great Britain.

3. When the settlers in Louisiana became angry with Spanish leaders, they started a _____ .

4. An important crop in the Louisiana territory was _____ .

5. The leaders of the United States wanted to control the _____ of the Mississippi River.

6. _____ forced Spain to return Louisiana to France.

Spotlight on People: Alexander O'Reilly

In the year 1769, Alexander O'Reilly was sent to Louisiana to end the rebellion. After O'Reilly ended the rebellion, he became governor. As the governor, he started to trade with the Native Americans. O'Reilly also set up a new government for the colony. He decided that all the settlers should speak Spanish, and he carried out Spanish laws.

O'Reilly set up a cabildo to help him govern. You learned that a cabildo is like a town council. O'Reilly stayed in Louisiana for only seven months. But by the time O'Reilly left in 1770, the Louisiana territory was at peace.

▲ Spain sent Alexander O'Reilly to end the rebellion in Louisiana.

SPANISH EXPLORERS DURING THE 1700s

LEARN NEW WORDS

Say each word. Write the word in the sentence.

desert (DEZ-urt)   1. A dry place where it rains very little is a _____ .

record (REK-urd)   2. When you write things in a diary to remember them, you are keeping a
_____ .

strait (STRAYT)   3. A narrow waterway that joins two large bodies of water is a
_____ .

LEARN A SKILL: Using Charts

On a **chart,** things are put into groups. The groups are listed in rows or in columns. To read a chart you read across (→) a row and down (↓) a column. Charts help you to look up and compare facts quickly.

Read the title of the chart on page 46. The title will tell you what you can find out on the chart. To look up something on this chart, you will have to read down (↓) and look across (→).

> **Hint:**
>
> Look across (→) a row and down (↓) a column.

Check (✔) your answers. Use the chart.

1. When did Eusebio Kino explore the Southwest?
   _____ 1691-1711
   _____ 1776
   _____ 1774-1775

2. Where did Juan Pérez explore?
   _____ Utah
   _____ Arizona
   _____ the northwest coast

3. When were parts of Colorado explored?
   _____ 1776
   _____ 1790
   _____ 1711

4. Did the chart help you find out what you wanted to know quickly?
   _____ Yes
   _____ No

MAKE PREDICTIONS

Read the title and headings. Use them to make predictions.

Put a (✔) mark next to the things you think you will learn about.

_____ who explored the Southwest

_____ where Cortés explored

_____ why Pérez made northwest claims

_____ where Anza led settlers

_____ which explorers kept records

_____ what voyages Malaspina made

The Spanish Explore the Southwest

1. You know the Spanish were busy settling the New World. Were they finished exploring there? Spanish exploration went on until the late 1700s. Many explorers were looking for better ways to travel through the new lands. Settlers, who came later, used these routes to travel more safely.

2. Between the years 1691 and 1711, a missionary, Father Eusebio Kino (KEE-noh), explored the **desert** areas of the Southwest. He built missions in Arizona. One mission he opened is still used as a church today. Kino also made maps of the places he explored. These maps helped Spanish explorers who came to these areas later.

▲ Eusebio Kino made 40 trips to southern Arizona.

Pérez Makes New Northwest Claims

3. During the middle of the 1700s, Spain learned that Russians were exploring the northwest coast of the New World. Spain worried that the Russians would take over this region. Spain sent Juan Pérez (PEH-rehs) to the northwest coast. He went to explore the area and to protect lands for Spain.

 REVIEW Why did Juan Pérez travel to the northwest coast?

4. On his first trip, Pérez sailed up the Pacific coast from California. Bad weather forced him to turn back. In 1775, Pérez tried again and made it up the coast. He explored parts of present-day Oregon and Washington. Pérez reached British Columbia and claimed the land for Spain.

Anza Leads Settlers to Monterey

5. In the year 1774, Juan Bautista de Anza (deh AHN-sah) looked for a good land route from Arizona to California. He reached present-day Monterey, California, on his first trip. Then he returned to Arizona.

6. In 1775, Anza set out for California again. Soldiers, their wives, missionaries, and other settlers went with him. They crossed the Colorado River on their way to Monterey. They built a cabin for missionaries along the river. The town of Yuma, Arizona, stands there today. Eight babies were born during this trip. One of these children was the first to be born of Spanish parents in California. Anza then set up the first presidio and mission in the area. It is now the city of San Francisco in California.

LOOK Look at the map on page 35. Find the city of San Francisco. Now find Monterey. Which city is farther north?

Explorers Keep Records

7. Silvestre Vélez de Escalante (VEH-lehs deh eh-skah-LAHN-teh), a missionary, tried to find a way from Santa Fe to Monterey. Bernardo Miera (mee-EHR-ah) went with him. Snow kept them from reaching California. But they did explore parts of Colorado, Utah, and northern Arizona. They were probably the first Europeans to see these lands.

8. During their 2,000-mile trip, Escalante kept a journal. Miera drew maps. Their journal and maps give a good **record** of their trip. People today read records like these to learn what it was like to explore these new lands.

TALK Do you write in a diary or journal? Imagine that someone will find your records in 200 years. Why would these records be interesting to them? Talk about it with your classmates.

Malaspina Makes New Voyages

9. In the year 1789, Alejandro Malaspina (mahl-uh-SPEEN-ah) sailed from Spain to South America. Scientists and artists went with him. They studied and kept records of things they found in the New World.

10. Then Malaspina sailed north to Alaska. He had heard stories about a northern waterway on the coast of Alaska that connected the Atlantic and Pacific oceans. Malaspina searched for a **strait** that would lead him to this waterway. He found a path of water leading toward the land. He tried to sail up this path, because he thought it was the strait. A **glacier**, or large piece of ice, blocked the way. Malaspina had been on a waterway that led into the land and then stopped. Malaspina learned that no waterway joined the two oceans. But he did give Spain its most northern claim on the Pacific coast.

REREAD What was Malaspina looking for along the Pacific coast?

SPANISH EXPLORERS DURING THE 1700s

Name	Dates	Explored
Eusebio Kino	1691-1711	Desert areas of the Southwest
Juan Pérez	1774-1775	The northwest coast, including British Columbia
Juan Bautista	1774-1775	A route from Arizona to Monterey, California
Silvestre Vélez de Escalante	1776	Parts of Colorado, Utah, and Arizona
Alejandro Malaspina	1790	The northern Pacific coast to Alaska

▲ This chart shows Spanish explorations made during the 1700s.

UNDERSTANDING WHAT YOU HAVE READ

Read the words in the box. Write the word that completes each sentence.

Russians	San Francisco
desert	records

1. Missionary Eusebio Kino explored the _____ areas of the Southwest.

2. Spain sent Juan Pérez to make sure that the _____ would not take over the northwest coast.

3. Juan Bautista de Anza found a way from Arizona to California and helped start the city of _____ .

4. Escalante and Miera kept _____ of their trip into Colorado, Utah, and northern Arizona.

Arts and Technology: Dress and Costume

Spanish people in the New World were very careful about the way they dressed. Wealthy Spanish wanted to make sure others knew they were rich. Wealthy men wore bright, colorful jackets. Their pants were made of velvet. Sometimes the men wore colorful blankets called **sarapes** (sah-RAH-pehs), placed over one shoulder. The rich women wore dresses made of silk and lace. They also wore **rebozos** (reh-BOH-sohs), which were long shawls of fine material. Sometimes the women wore fine jewels.

Whenever they could, rich Spanish settlers wore clothes that came from Europe. They did not think fine clothes made in the New World were as good.

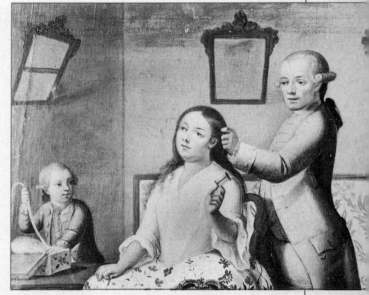

▲ Rich Spanish colonists dressed like this. The family wears fine clothing. The boy holds jewels for his mother.

DAILY LIFE IN THE SPANISH COLONIES

LEARN NEW WORDS

Say each word. Write the word in the sentence.

culture (KUL-chur)

language (LANG-gwij)

customs (KUS-tumz)

1. Arts, religion, and beliefs make up a people's _____ .

2. The words we use to speak and to write are called our
    _____ .

3. When we follow the usual behaviors of a country, we follow its
    _____ .

LEARN A SKILL: Finding the Main Idea and Details

You know that a **main idea** sentence gives the important idea in a reading.
A **detail** sentence tells more about the main idea.

Find paragraph 7 on page 50. Write the sentence that gives the main idea.
Then write the detail sentences.

Main Idea: _____

_____

Details: _____

_____

_____

In this paragraph, the main idea sentence is

_____ the first sentence. _____ in the middle. _____ the last sentence.

MAKE PREDICTIONS

Read the title and headings. Use them to make predictions.

Put a (✔) mark next to the things you think you will learn about.

_____ about Spanish culture

_____ why missions were important

_____ how Native Americans changed

_____ what life was like in Spain

_____ about a new class system

_____ how colonies were different

48

OBJECTIVE: Read to find out what life was like for the Spanish settlers in the New World.

TIP: Finding main ideas and details will help you.

Spanish Culture in the New World

1. Imagine you live in Spain. You are moving to the New World. Your ship will leave soon. You have packed your bags. You will bring your Spanish books, clothes, and other things with you.

2. Spanish settlers brought their Spanish **culture** to the colonies. Their culture was made up of their **language**, their **customs**, and their religion. The settlers wanted to live in the New World. But they wanted the New World to be like Spain. They even called the parts of the New World they settled in "New Spain."

REVIEW

What things made up the Spanish culture in the New World? Hint: The second sentence in paragraph 2 will help you.

3. The Spanish settlers built **communities** in the New World. A community is a group of people that live near each other. People in a community share the same way of life. They also share many of the same interests and customs.

Missions Are Important

4. Missions were important to the Spanish way of life in the New World. A mission was often the center of life in a community. Not only was the mission the church, it was also used as a school for children in the community. The land around the mission was used as farm land to grow food.

▲ This is a drawing of New Orleans in the 1700s. The church in the drawing is in the center of the city. Churches and missions were often at the center of Spanish colonial towns and cities.

5. Missions in the Spanish colonies were similar to each other. Usually, other parts of the community were built around the mission. A presidio was built near the mission to protect the community. Spanish soldiers lived in the presidio. Small pueblos often were located around the missions. The Spanish settlers lived in these pueblos. Review the picture map of San Antonio on page 32 in Lesson 7. This is how a Spanish community looked.

6. Each day in the community began with church services at the mission. These services included marriages and other religious events. After breakfast, the Native Americans worked on the mission farm lands. The workers then ate lunch, and then farmed again until dinner time. At night, the people had time to dance, sing songs, and play games.

New Ways for Native Americans

7. The Spanish culture changed the Native American way of life. Spanish priests at the mission taught Native Americans about the Christian religion. Priests also taught them to read and write in the Spanish language. The Native Americans also learned about Spanish customs.

8. Native American men and boys farmed the mission land. They grew crops from Europe, such as wheat and rice. They also grew American crops, such as corn, beans, and squash. Native Americans took care of the cattle and sheep that the settlers brought.

9. Native American women learned new crafts and how to cook new types of meals. Soon a new way of cooking began. This new way mixed Spanish and American ways of cooking food.

 TALK Talk about how the Native American way of life changed after the Spanish settled in the New World.

A New Class System Begins

10. A new **class system** became part of life in the New World. In a class system, some people are thought to be more important than others. A person's importance in the class system was based on background. Background means where a person was born and who their parents were.

11. The most important people in this system were those born in Spain to Spanish parents. They were called **peninsulares** (peh-NEEN-soo-lah-res). The next class were the **criollos** (kree-OH-yohs), children born in America to Spanish parents. Criollos were not treated as well as peninsulares. **Mestizos** (meh-STEE-sohs) were next in importance. Mestizos were people who had both Spanish and Native American backgrounds. Native Americans came last, unless Blacks lived in the community. Free Blacks and slaves came after Native Americans in the class system.

REREAD Which class of people had Spanish and Native American parents?

Differences Among Colonies

12. There were some differences among the Spanish colonies in the New World. At St. Augustine, Florida, the settlers raised crops and cattle. The community had to protect itself from attacks by pirates. The settlers at San Antonio, Texas lived by farming and hunting. They had to worry about attacks from the Native Americans.

▲ People of mixed Spanish and Native American background were called mestizos.

50

CHECK THE OBJECTIVE: Write down in your notebook one thing that tells what life was like when the Spanish settlers moved to the colonies.

UNDERSTANDING WHAT YOU HAVE READ

Read the words in the box. Write the word that completes each sentence.

communities	culture	mission
mestizos	class system	

1. The Spanish settlers' language, customs, and religion made up their

    _____ .

2. The Spanish settlers lived near each other in _____ .

3. A community's church and school were both in the _____ .

4. People who had both Spanish and Native American backgrounds were

    _____ .

5. When some people are thought to be more important than others in a community, it is called _____ .

Spotlight on People: Sor Juana Inés de la Cruz

Sor (or Sister) Juana Inés de la Cruz (ee-NES deh lah KROOS) was born in a Mexican village in the year 1651. She became one of the greatest Hispanic poets.

Sor Inés de la Cruz learned to read when she was three years old. By the time she was eight, she was writing poems. She wanted to go to the University of Mexico. But the school would not let her in. Girls and women were not allowed to study there. Sor Inés de la Cruz moved to Mexico City when she was nine. There she became famous as a poet and a student.

Later, Sor Inés de la Cruz became a nun. She made money by selling the books she owned. She gave this money away to poor people.

▲ Sor Juana Inés de la Cruz was one of the first great Hispanic poets.

THE AMERICAN REVOLUTION

LEARN NEW WORDS

Say each word. Write the word in the sentence.

port (PORT)

1. A place along a coast where ships load and unload goods is called a
_____ .

capture (KAP-chur)

2. To take something by force and win control over it is to
_____ it.

declare (dih-KLAIR)

3. A country can _____ war on another country.

LEARN A SKILL: Using Time Lines

As you have read, a **time line** shows the order in which things happen.
Thinking about time when you read will help you understand history.

Find the time line on page 54. Write the title.

_____

Read the events shown on the time line. Then answer the questions.

1. When did Spain declare war on Great Britain? _____

2. When was the U.S. Declaration of Independence signed? _____

3. What happened in the year 1781? _____

4. What did Great Britain return to Spain in the year 1783? _____

MAKE PREDICTIONS

Read the title and headings. Use them to make predictions.

Put a (✔) mark next to the things you think you will learn about.

_____ how the Europeans helped

_____ who went to Spain

_____ when the Spanish king died

_____ what help the Spanish sent

_____ what ways the Cubans helped

_____ how Gálvez fought the British

OBJECTIVE: Read to find out how Spain and its colonies helped the Americans fight their war for independence.

TIP: Reading time lines can help you find out.

WHILE YOU READ

Lesson 12

Europeans Help the Americans

1. In 1776, the 13 American colonies were fighting for independence from Great Britain. This war was the American Revolution. To win the war, the colonists needed help. Both France and Spain agreed to send the Americans money. Each country gave great amounts of money. Spain continued to send money during the war.

2. Spain helped the Americans in other ways. A Spanish company sent guns and other supplies. Spanish soldiers came to America to help fight the war. And Spain let American ships use **ports** in Spain and in its Spanish colonies.

REREAD How did Spain help the Americans during the war?

Spanish Colonies Send Help

3. The Spanish colonies also wanted to help. Like Spain, the colonies sent soldiers to

▲ Bernardo de Gálvez helped the American colonists win the war for independence.

help the Americans fight. In California, Father Junípero Serra collected money for the Americans. He got money from both Spanish settlers and Native Americans.

4. Bernardo de Gálvez, the governor of Louisiana, also wanted to help the Americans. He sent food, medicine, and guns to the American settlers. He let American ships use the port in New Orleans. Gálvez **captured** the British ships that tried to use the port. He ordered all British people to leave Louisiana.

Cubans Find Many Ways to Help

5. You know that Cuba is an island off Florida. Many Cubans disliked the British. Why? The British had captured the city of Havana, Cuba, from Spain in the year 1762. They controlled the city for a year. They caused the Cuban people a lot of suffering. Then in the year 1763, the British took Florida from Spain. At the same time, they gave Havana, Cuba, back to Spain. Spanish settlers then fled from Florida to Cuba. So, many Cubans wanted the American colonists to win the war against Great Britain.

REVIEW Why did many Cubans dislike the British?

6. Juan Manuel de Cagigal (deh kah-jih-GAHL) was the governor of Cuba during the American Revolution. Cagigal told his people that the Americans needed money. American soldiers needed food, clothes, and other supplies. The rich women of Havana gave most of the money. The women even gave away their jewelry!

7. The Cubans helped the Americans in other ways, too. They let American ships use the ports in Havana. The Cubans also repaired American ships for free.

8. Juan de Miralles (deh mee-RAH-yes) was a rich Spanish merchant. He had lived in Havana for many years. Miralles helped pay for the repairs of the American ships. He wanted Cuba to trade more with the 13 colonies. In the year 1778, Miralles traveled to America. He met with American leaders. He even became good friends with George Washington. Miralles worked to get Spain to **declare** war on Great Britain.

Use the time line. In which year did Miralles work to get Spain to declare war on Great Britain?

Gálvez Fights the British

9. In the year 1779, Spain did declare war on Great Britain. Spain was still angry at he British for capturing Florida. Spain hoped to get Florida back from the British. Spain also wanted the British to leave their ports in the Gulf of Mexico.

10. Do you remember Bernardo de Gálvez, the Spanish governor of Louisiana? In the year 1779, he attacked British forts along the Mississippi River. Gálvez also attacked the British ports in the Gulf of Mexico. The most important attack was in the year 1781, at Pensacola, Florida.

11. Gálvez helped weaken the British Army. The British lost all their forts on the Mississippi River. They lost their ports in the Gulf of Mexico. By defeating the British, Gálvez helped the Americans win the war. In the year 1783, Great Britain and America agreed to end the war. Great Britain also returned the territory of Florida to Spain.

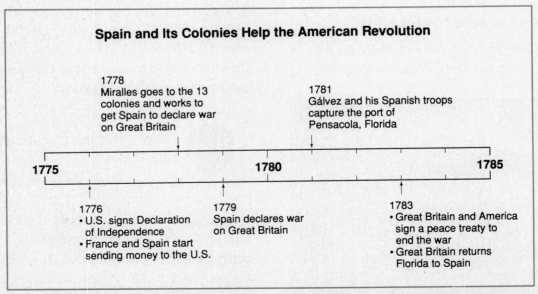

Spain and Its Colonies Help the American Revolution

1778
Miralles goes to the 13 colonies and works to get Spain to declare war on Great Britain

1781
Gálvez and his Spanish troops capture the port of Pensacola, Florida

1775   1780   1785

1776
• U.S. signs Declaration of Independence
• France and Spain start sending money to the U.S.

1779
Spain declares war on Great Britain

1783
• Great Britain and America sign a peace treaty to end the war
• Great Britain returns Florida to Spain

▲ This time line shows events in the order they happened. Test yourself: What is the date of the first event shown on this time line?

CHECK THE OBJECTIVE: **Write in your notebook one way Spain and its colonies helped the Americans fight the war for independence.**

UNDERSTANDING WHAT YOU HAVE READ

Read each pair of sentences. Underline the sentence that is <u>true</u>.

1. Spain sent money to help the Americans fight their war.
   France and Spain refused to send money to the Americans.

2. People in the Spanish colonies helped the British fight.
   People in the Spanish colonies helped the Americans fight.

3. Cuban women were not interested in the American war.
   Cuban women gave away their jewelry to help the Americans.

4. Gálvez captured British forts along the Mississippi River.
   Gálvez captured British forts along the Missouri River.

5. The British lost all of Florida in a fight led by Gálvez.
   The British lost the port of Pensacola in a fight led by Gálvez.

Spotlight on People: Bernardo de Gálvez

Bernardo de Gálvez was born in Spain in the year 1746. He was made governor of Louisiana about the same time the American Revolution began. Gálvez helped America fight against the British in many ways. His most important fight was at Pensacola in Florida. Gálvez knew Pensacola would be hard to capture because it had strong forts. To reach Pensacola, Gálvez had to sail into Pensacola Bay. An island blocked the entrance to the bay.

Gálvez carefully planned his attack on Pensacola. He went to Havana to get men and ships. He returned with 7,000 soldiers. He led a small group of them to the island in Pensacola Bay. Then he sailed his ships into the bay. Meanwhile, the men on the island went into Pensacola on smaller boats. The plan worked! On May 10, 1781, the British gave up Pensacola.

▲ Gálvez led the Spanish soldiers in the attack at Pensacola.

SPANISH COLONIES AFTER 1783

LEARN NEW WORDS

Say each word. Write the word in the sentence.

depot (DEP-oh)

integrated (IN-tuh-grayt-ed)

range (RAYNJ)

1. A place where supplies are kept is a _____ .

2. A school attended by students of different races is _____ .

3. An open area of land where cattle live is a _____ .

LEARN A SKILL: Taking Notes

Notes will help you remember what you read. There are three steps to taking good notes:

> • Turn headings into questions.
>
> • Read.
>
> • Write answers to the questions.

You already know how to turn headings into questions. To do the second step, read to find the answer to the question you wrote. To do step three, write the answer as soon as you find it.

Read paragraph 7 under the heading "A new School Opens".
Take good notes. Remember to follow the three steps.

Question: _____

Answer/Notes: _____

_____

_____

MAKE PREDICTIONS

Read the title and headings. Use them to make predictions.

Put a (✔) mark next to the things you think you will learn about.

_____ when the British had Florida

_____ why the Spanish returned

_____ where settlers came from

_____ why a new school opened

_____ how Americans won their war

_____ what vaqueros did on ranches

OBJECTIVE: Read to find out about life in Spanish colonies in Florida and in the Southwest after the year 1783.

TIP: Taking notes as you read will help you.

The British Control Florida

1. Remember that Britain took over Florida in 1763. Most Spanish settlers left Florida when it became British. For 20 years, British settlers set up British colonies in Florida. They built roads and buildings. One British man started Florida's first newspaper.

2. What happened when the American Revolution began? St. Augustine, Florida, became an important city to the British. It was a **depot** for British troops. Guns and army supplies were kept in the depot. The British kept the captured American soldiers in St. Augustine. Many American colonists who wanted the British to win, also lived there.

REVIEW

Why was St. Augustine important to the British during the war? Hint: Paragraph 2 will help you.

The Spanish Return to Florida

3. In the year 1783, Spain took over Florida again. The American Revolution was over, and the British had lost the war. The British agreed to leave Florida.

4. Florida got a new Spanish governor. He was Vicente Manuel de Zéspedes (deh SEHS-peh-dehs) from Cuba. Zéspedes came to St. Augustine with 500 soldiers in 1784. Many settlers returned to Florida with him, too. Other Spanish settlers had stayed in Florida while it was under British rule.

▲When Governor Zéspedes arrived in St. Augustine, he lived in the Governor's House. To help Florida grow, Zéspedes let settlers who were not Spanish or Catholic move into the region. Zéspedes left Florida in 1790, due to his poor health.

Settlers Come to St. Augustine

5. The people of St. Augustine, Florida, came from many lands and cultures. They spoke many different languages. The settlers were not only from Spain. They came from Italy, Greece, Switzerland, Germany, and other European countries. Many Blacks also lived in St. Augustine. Most Blacks in St. Augustine were slaves, but some were free.

6. The largest group of settlers came to St. Augustine from Minorca, Spain. Minorca is an island off the east coast of Spain. Great Britain had taken Minorca from Spain. In the year 1783, the British returned the island to Spain.

A New School Opens

7. In the year 1787, a new school was opened in St. Augustine. The school was set

up by a priest named Father Thomas Hassett. It was not like mission schools in the Southwest. In those schools, priests taught Native Americans in separate classes from Spanish children. This school was special. The new school was the first **integrated** public school in the United States. This meant that children of different races could attend the school together. The first teacher of the school was Cuban-born Father Francisco Traconis (trah-KOH-nees). The school was closed in the year 1821.

 REREAD Why was the school in St. Augustine special? Hint: Read sentences 5 and 6 to find out.

Raising Cattle in the Southwest

8. What was life like in the Spanish colonies in the Southwest? As you know, most settlements were built around missions. But cattle raising was becoming a very important way of life. Ranchers were trying a new way to raise cattle. The cattle were no longer kept inside fences all year. Ranchers let their cattle live out on the **range**. Then cattle could move freely to feed for most of the year. This new way of raising cattle began in Mexico. Then it spread to Texas, the Southwest, and California.

Vaqueros Work on Ranchos

9. Vaqueros worked on the new ranchos, or large farms. Their job was to protect the cattle. Vaqueros did most of their work on horseback. They rode out on the range with the cattle. Vaqueros became very skilled at riding horses.

10. Sometimes the vaqueros held contests. During these contests, they would ride horses and throw ropes to catch cattle. The vaqueros liked to see who had the best skills. These contests became known as **rodeos** (roh-DEH-ohs). This Spanish word is also used in our language. We say it differently (ROH-dee-ohs).

 TALK Would you like to be a vaquero in a rodeo? Why or why no? Talk it over with your classmates.

11. Soon another change came to the Southwest. The new U.S. nation only went as far west as the Rocky Mountains. But Americans from the new nation were moving farther west. They were settling in lands owned and ruled by Spain.

▲ This picture shows Native American boys being taught at a mission school in the Southwest.

CHECK THE OBJECTIVE: Write in your notebook how life changed in Spanish colonies in Florida and in the Southwest after the year 1783.

UNDERSTANDING WHAT YOU HAVE READ

Find the correct answer to each question. Circle the letter.

1. Who took control of Florida in 1763?
   a. the American colonists
   b. the Spanish
   c. the British

2. When did the Spanish settlers return to Florida?
   a. when the British moved to Cuba
   b. when the British gave Florida back to Spain
   c. when Spain fought against the U.S.

3. What was special about the new school, set up in 1787, in St. Augustine?
   a. It was started by a priest.
   b. It was integrated.
   c. It was in Florida.

4. What job did the vaqueros have?
   a. They held contests for fun.
   b. They owned the ranchos.
   c. They protected the cattle.

Using Primary Sources: Rules at Public School

The first integrated public school in the U.S. opened in St. Augustine, Florida. The students had to follow a set of rules. Here are some of those rules.

5. Throughout the year the schools shall be opened at seven o'clock in the morning and at two in the afternoon. At no time shall the pupils be dismissed in the morning before twelve o'clock, nor in the afternoon in winter before sunset . . . .

10. The school rooms shall be swept at least once a week by the pupils . . . .

12. . . . [T]o the first or most capable of each class shall be given some title, reserving for the first of the highest class the title of Emperor . . . .

13. Every month there shall be a general examination before the parish priest and the teachers to determine the advancement the pupils may have made . . . in writing, reading, arithmetic, Christian doctrine, etc . . . .

14. From pupils studying the alphabet, the syllabary, and reading, the teacher shall hear four lessons a day, two in the morning and two in the afternoon . . . .

15. Pupils in arithmetic or counting shall solve two problems a day, write one or two exercises, read two lessons and receive instructions in Christian doctrine once in the afternoon . . . .

SUMMARY OF LESSONS 9-13

Here are some important ideas you learned in Lessons 9-13. Write the one you want to remember.

- Louisiana was ruled by Spain for 30 years, from 1763 to 1800. (9)

- Spanish explorers started new settlements along the northwest coast until the late 1700s. (10)

- Spanish settlers brought their culture to Native Americans in the New World. (11)

- Spain and the Spanish colonies helped British colonies in their war for independence. (12)

- In 1783, settlers from many countries came to live in Florida. (13)

- In the Southwest, vaqueros protected cattle on large ranges, or ranchos. (13)

REVIEWING NEW WORDS

Look up the words below in the Glossary. Write the correct word in each sentence.

culture (11)	captured (12)	desert (10)
range (13)	official (9)	integrated (13)

1. A _____ is a dry place where there is little rain.

2. The settlers' _____ was made up of their language, customs, and religion.

3. The first _____ public school in the U.S. opened in 1787.

4. Spain became the _____ ruler of Louisiana in the 1763.

5. Cattle live and feed on an open area of land called a _____ .

6. The British _____ the city of Havana in 1762.

REVIEWING WHAT YOU HAVE READ

Read the words in the box. Write the words that complete each sentence.

Minorca	**duties**	**northwest**
mestizos	**Pensacola**	**rancheros**

1. Bernardo de Gálvez helped the Americans win the war for independence by attacking the British port of _____ .

2. Settlers in Louisiana disliked Governor Ulloa because he made them pay _____ .

3. People who had both Spanish and Native American backgrounds were called _____ .

4. Spain sent Juan Pérez to the _____ coast to protect land from the Russians.

5. The rich owners of new cattle ranches were called _____ .

6. The largest group of settlers in St. Augustine came from the island of _____ , near Spain.

REVIEWING SKILLS

Study the map.

Write **T** if the sentence is true. Write **F** if the sentence is false.

_____ 1. Most of the Spanish attacks took place along the Mississippi River.

_____ 2. On the map, British land is in the color gray.

_____ 3. The attack farthest to the north was at Natchez.

British Forts Attacked in the American Revolution

Fort St. Joseph

St. Louis □ Cahokia
□ Fort Charles
LOUISIANA □ Kaskaskia

Mississippi River

FLORIDA
(British from
1763-1783)

□ Nogales
Mobile
TEXAS □ Natchez
Pensacola
Baton Rouge □
Manchac □

New Orleans

GULF OF MEXICO

■ Land claimed by Spain
□ Land claimed by Great Britain
□ British fort

HISPANICS DURING THE EARLY 1800s

LEARN NEW WORDS

Say each word. Write the word in the sentence.

traditions (truh-DISH-unz)

1. Customs passed down from parents to children make up a family's _____ .

battle (BAT-ul)

2. A fight between two countries at war is called a _____ .

treaty (TREET-ee)

3. When two countries want to end a war, they sign an agreement, or _____ .

LEARN A SKILL: SQ3R

Let's say you are going to have a test on Monday. You can use a study plan called **SQ3R** to get ready for the test.

The words in dark type tell what SQ3R stands for.

- **Survey** means to look at the headings, title, pictures, and maps.

- **Question** means to turn every heading into a question.

- **Read** the part to find the answer to the question.

- **Recite** means to say the answer to yourself.

- **Review** means to go back over the whole reading. Say the questions again and try to answer them.

Use SQ3R as you read Lesson 14. Then answer the question.

I found SQ3R to be _____ helpful. _____ not helpful.

MAKE PREDICTIONS

Read the title and headings. Use them to make predictions.

Put a (✔) mark next to the things you think you will learn about.

_____ who Hispanics and Latinos were

_____ why Hispanics were in the war

_____ Hispanics in the 20th century

_____ who won the final battle

_____ when Hispanics came to the U.S.

_____ the first mission in Mexico

Hispanic and Latino People

1. Early Spanish colonists in the Americas were from Spain. They spoke Spanish. They brought their Spanish **traditions** to the New World. But what about family members born in the New World? They were not really Spanish since they were not born in Spain.

2. By the 1800s, most people who spoke Spanish in the Americas were not from Spain. At one time, there was no name for these people. Today they are called **Hispanico** (ee-SPAH-nee-koh) or **Latino** (lah-TEE-noh) people. Hispanico is **Hispanic** (his-PAN-ik) in English.

3. Hispanics are not the only people who are named for their background. North Americans who speak English are called **Anglos**. This word means "English." But most of these people are not from England. They, or their parents, might have come from other European countries. But these people are called Anglos because they speak English. In the same way, people are called Hispanics because they speak Spanish or have Spanish traditions.

 REVIEW What is the background of a Hispanic person?

Hispanics in the United States

4. What were some of the different Hispanic groups in the Americas? One small group was the **Sephardic** (suh-FARD-ik) Jews. The word Sephardic comes from the Hebrew word for Spain. In 1654, a group of Sephardic Jews left their homes in Brazil. They moved to New Amsterdam, now called New York City. The **ancestors** of these people had left Spain in 1492. Why had they left?

5. In 1492, the king and queen of Spain decided only Christians could be Spanish. Jews and Muslims living in Spain had to become Christians or leave. The Sephardic Jews refused to be converted. Instead, they left Spain. Some moved to the New World. Many Sephardic Jews had Spanish names. And, they

► One popular dance in the Spanish colonies during the 1800s was the **fandango** (fan-DAHN-goh). The music for this dance probably came from the Spanish colonies in the late 1600s. People in Spain heard about the dance and learned to do it, too.

spoke a language similar to Spanish, called **Ladino** (lah-DEE-noh).

 Why did the Sephardic Jews have to leave Spain in 1492?

6. By the year 1800, many criollos, mestizos, and **mulatos** (muh-LAH-tohs) had moved to new places in the Americas. <u>Mulato</u> is a Spanish word for a person with parents of European and African background. Remember that criollos were people born in the Americas to Spanish parents. Mestizos had Spanish and Native American parents. These Hispanic people often spoke Spanish and had Spanish traditions.

 What traditions do you keep that come from your family background? Tell your classmates about them.

Hispanics in the War of 1812

7. The War of 1812 began between the United States and Great Britain. What was it about? Great Britain controlled travel on the seas. The U.S. fought for the freedom to sail and trade with whomever it pleased. Also, the U.S. wanted Great Britain to stop forcing American sailors to work on British ships.

8. Hispanics in the U.S. helped fight several **battles** against Great Britain. They helped even though Spain was on Great Britain's side in the war. One Hispanic fighter was Jorge Ferragut (FEHR-uh-gut). He had fought in the American Revolution many years earlier. Although Ferragut was in his fifties, he fought for the United States again. His young son, David, was an American sailor. He fought in battles against the British, too.

 In what two wars did Jorge Ferragut fight for the United States?

9. In 1814, the United States and Great Britain signed a **treaty**. The Treaty of Ghent (GENT) ended the war. The U.S. had hoped to win Canada and Florida. But the treaty did not give either country any new land.

A Final Battle Is Fought

10. The British and United States armies fought one last battle after the Treaty of Ghent was signed in December 1814. News of the signing traveled slowly. The last, large battle took place in New Orleans, Louisiana, in January 1815.

11. This Battle of New Orleans was led by General Andrew Jackson. Hispanics from New Orleans helped him fight the British in this battle. On January 8, 1815, Jackson won the Battle of New Orleans. More than 2,000 British soldiers died. Only 21 soldiers from the United States died or were hurt. The Battle of New Orleans made Jackson an American hero.

▲ This picture shows the Battle of New Orleans that was fought in the War of 1812. Hispanic settlers helped General Andrew Jackson win this battle.

CHECK THE OBJECTIVE: **Write in your notebook a sentence that tells who Hispanic people are.**

UNDERSTANDING WHAT YOU HAVE READ

Read. Write the letter to match.

_____ **1.** Sephardic Jews

_____ **2.** Andrew Jackson

_____ **3.** Battle of New Orleans

_____ **4.** Treaty of Ghent

_____ **5.** mulatos

_____ **6.** Hispanics

a. a general and a hero in the War of 1812

b. refused to become Christians and left Spain

c. the last, big fight of the War of 1812

d. signed to end the War of 1812

e. people with European and African backgrounds

f. people who speak Spanish or have Spanish traditions

Arts and Technology: Arts and Handicrafts

In the 1800s, many arts and handicrafts were developed in New Mexico. Some artists made religious carvings. People wanted these religious carvings, or statues, for their homes and churches. The statues were usually of a saint or a religious scene. Today, art collectors pay a lot of money to buy these carvings.

Jewelry-making was another important art. Skilled workers made gold and silver jewelry. Often the jewelry had lacy designs known as **filigree**. Filigree jewelry has open spaces between the gold or silver. The art of making filigree jewelry came from Spain.

▲ This piece of filigree jewelry was made in New Mexico.

THE UNITED STATES GAINS FLORIDA

LEARN NEW WORDS

Say each word. Write the word in the sentence.

purchase (PUR-chus)

border (BORD-ur)

trial (TRYL)

1. When you buy a sweater, you _____ it.

2. A line on a map that divides land owned by two countries is called the _____ .

3. To decide whether a person has broken the law, the person is given a _____ in court.

LEARN A SKILL: Using Maps

You know that a **map** is a drawing of a real place. Maps can help you answer questions about where things happened.

Find the map on page 68. Write the title.

_____

Use the map to answer the questions.

1. What is the name of the area colored dark green? _____

2. Which river forms the border between East Florida and West Florida? _____

3. By what year did St. Augustine become part of the United States? _____

4. Which city became part of the United States first: St. Marks or Mobile? _____

MAKE PREDICTIONS

Read the title and headings. Use them to make predictions.

Put a (✔) mark next to the things you think you will learn about.

_____ why the United States wanted Florida

_____ how Spain lost West Florida

_____ what war Spain fought in Europe

_____ what the Seminoles wanted

_____ whom Jackson attacked

_____ why Spain signed the treaty

The United States Wants Florida

1. More than one nation wanted to control Florida. Spain had once controlled it. Then Great Britain controlled Florida during the years 1763-1783. In 1783, Spain got control of Florida again.

2. The United States also wanted to own Florida. The British had divided Florida into East Florida and West Florida. In 1803, Thomas Jefferson tried to **purchase** West Florida. He wanted to purchase it when he bought Louisiana. But Jefferson's plan was not successful.

REREAD Was West Florida part of the Louisiana Purchase?

3. In 1810, a group of Americans moved into West Florida. They captured the Spanish fort at Baton Rouge (BAT-un ROOJ). They declared West Florida a **republic**. In a republic, people vote for their leaders. A republic is not ruled by a king. By calling West Florida a republic, the Americans could ignore the rule of the Spanish king.

Spain Loses West Florida

4. In October 1810, President James Madison declared that the United States controlled part of West Florida. He said the land from the Mississippi River to the Perdido River was under American control. Spain did not like this claim. But Spain was busy fighting a war in Europe. Spain could not fight against the United States, too.

▲ The Americans finally gained East Florida. This drawing shows the fort at St. Augustine as the Spanish were leaving. The Spanish soldiers fired the cannons before lowering the Spanish flag for the last time.

5. In the year 1813, the United States captured the Spanish fort at Mobile. The U.S. took over the rest of West Florida that year. Could Spain keep its control over East Florida much longer?

Seminoles Want Their Land Back

6. Problems with the Seminole (SEM-uh-nohl) people were occurring in East Florida. The Seminoles were Native Americans. They had moved from land in the United States to the Spanish colony of Florida. But they wanted their land back from the U.S. The Seminoles camped along the **border** between the U.S. and East Florida. They crossed the border into the U.S. to attack American settlers. Then the Seminoles came back across the border to safety in the Spanish colony of East Florida.

REVIEW — What problem was there with the Seminoles in East Florida?

LOOK — On which body of water is St. Marks in East Florida located?

7. The U.S. government wanted the Seminoles to stop the attacks. The Americans did not want to return any land to the Seminoles. Instead, the U.S. government sent troops to chase the Seminoles back across the border. The Seminoles were forced into the Spanish territory of East Florida.

Jackson Attacks the Seminoles

8. In 1818, General Andrew Jackson attacked the Seminoles who had crossed the border into Georgia. He followed them back into East Florida. Jackson captured the Spanish fort of St. Marks in East Florida. His troops captured two Seminole leaders and two British fur traders. They accused these four people of giving **weapons** to the Seminoles. The two Seminole leaders were killed without a **trial**. The British traders were killed after their trials. Jackson also forced the Spanish governor to leave office.

9. Most Americans were pleased with Jackson's attacks. Spain was angry. John Quincy Adams, the U.S. Secretary of State, blamed Spain. He said the Spanish were encouraging the Seminoles to attack. Adams told Spain to control the Seminoles or give up East Florida.

Spain Signs a Treaty

10. Adams and a Spanish official named Luis de Onís (deh oh-NEES) worked on a treaty. The Adams-Onís Treaty was signed by Spain and the U.S. to solve their problems. The treaty said that East Florida and West Florida belonged to the U.S. Spain also gave up its claim to land in Oregon. In return, the United States gave up any claim to Texas.

11. The United States signed the Adams-Onís Treaty in 1819. Spain signed it in 1821. After Spain signed the treaty, all of Florida finally belonged to the United States.

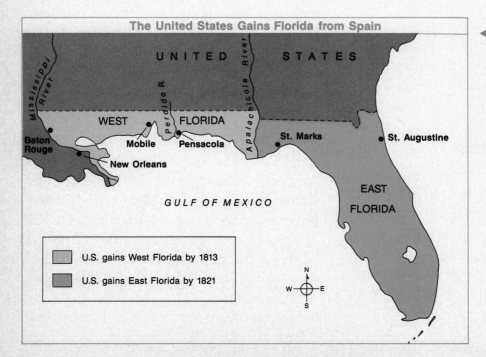

This map shows when the United States gained West Florida and East Florida. Test yourself: By what year did Pensacola become part of the United States? Use the map key to help you.

68

CHECK THE OBJECTIVE: **Write one sentence in your notebook that tells how the U. S. gained control of West Florida and another that tells when the U.S. gained control of East Florida.**

AFTER YOU READ

Lesson **15**

UNDERSTANDING WHAT YOU HAVE READ

Read each pair of sentences. Underline the sentence that is <u>true</u>.

1. The United States wanted to own Florida.
   The United States wanted Spain to keep Florida.

2. Jefferson bought West Florida as part of the Louisiana Purchase.
   West Florida was not part of the Louisiana Purchase.

3. The Seminoles were Spanish settlers who wanted their U.S. land back.
   The Seminoles were Native Americans who wanted their U.S. land back.

4. Spain gave up Florida by signing a treaty.
   Spain gave up Florida by losing the land in a war.

Spotlight on People: Joseph Hernández

When the territory of Florida became part of the United States, it needed leaders. Joseph Hernández (ehr-NAHN-des) was one of Florida's new leaders.

Hernández was born in Florida. His parents came to Florida from Minorca in Spain in 1768. Hernández owned a large farm. He also worked as an official for the city of St. Augustine. Then he became the mayor of St. Augustine.

In 1822, Hernández went to Washington, D.C. He was the first Hispanic member of the United States **Congress**. In Congress, Hernández could share his ideas with the other members, but he could not vote. Only members from states could vote, and Florida was not yet a state. Hernández also served as president of the Territorial Legislature. Hernández left Washington, D.C., and returned to Florida in 1845.

▲ Joseph Hernández was the first Hispanic leader in Congress.

MEXICO AND ITS INDEPENDENCE

LEARN NEW WORDS

Say each word. Write the word in the sentence.

revolution (rev-uh-LOO-shun)

1. A fight to change the government of a country is called a _____ .

emperor (EM-pur-ur)

2. The ruler of a country or empire is called an _____ .

representative (rep-rih-ZENT-ut-iv)

3. A government in which people choose their leaders is called a _____ government.

LEARN A SKILL: Summarizing

When you read history, you can talk about the important, or main, ideas. **Summarizing** is telling the main ideas. Remember:

* A summary is very short.

* A summary gives the main ideas.

When you have finished reading "Mexico and Its Independence," come back to this page. Fill in the missing parts of the summary.

Mexico wanted its _____ from Spain. Mexico fought

a _____ to gain its freedom. Mexico became

independent in the year _____ . In 1824, Mexico became

a _____ . President James Monroe presented the

_____ . The U.S. promised to protect new countries in

the Americas from European countries.

MAKE PREDICTIONS

Read the title and headings. Use them to make predictions.

Put a (✔) mark next to the things you think you will learn about.

_____ how Aztecs lived in Mexico   _____ who lived in New Spain

_____ why Mexico wanted independence   _____ when Mexico became a republic

_____ where Hidalgo led the fighters   _____ what the Monroe Doctrine was

Mexico Wants Independence

1. By the year 1790, Europe had ruled colonies in the Americas for about 300 years. These colonies were unhappy under European rule. They wanted their independence. There were many **revolutions** in Central America and South America from the years 1791 to 1824. Like the American Revolution against Great Britain, these were fights for independence. The Mexican Revolution began in 1810.

2. Mexico's fight for freedom was begun by Father Miguel Hidalgo y Costilla (ee-DAHL-goh ee kos-TEE-yah). Hidalgo was a criollo priest in the town of Dolores. On September 16, 1810, Father Hidalgo called the people of Dolores to the church. He demanded that the Spanish end their rule over Mexico. He said Spain should return the land to the Native Americans.

▲ This painting shows Father Miguel Hidalgo. He began Mexico's fight for independence from Spain.

Hidalgo Leads First Fighters

3. Hidalgo gathered together an army of Native Americans to fight the Spanish. Hidalgo's army captured two Mexican towns. Then Hidalgo and about 80,000 men attacked Spanish government troops near Mexico City. Hidalgo's army won the first battle. Another hero of the Mexican Revolution was María Josefa Ortiz de Domínguez (or-TEES deh doh-MEENG-es). She warned Father Hidalgo that he might get caught. (María Ortiz is pictured on the cover of this book, at left, in a red dress.) Hidalgo tried to escape, but he was captured and killed. Hidalgo's idea of freedom for Mexico lived on.

TALK

Most towns in Mexico have a street or a park named after Father Hidalgo. Why do you think this is so?

4. Another priest who fought for Mexico's freedom was Father José María Morelos (moh-REH-los). He continued the fight against Spain. Morelos and his men won many battles against the Spanish. In 1813, Morelos declared Mexico an independent country. He started a new government. But the criollos did not want him as their leader. They turned against him. In 1815, Morelos was captured and killed.

Mexico Becomes a Republic

5. From the years 1815 to 1820, the Mexican Revolution slowed down. But Vicente Guerrero (gehr-REH-roh) continued the fight with small groups of men. In the year

1820, **royalists**, supporters of the Spanish king, wanted to stop Guerrero. They sent Agustín de Iturbide (deh ee-toor-BEE-deh) to stop the revolution.

6. Iturbide changed his mind about the revolution and joined Guerrero. These two leaders had a lot of support from the Mexicans. Only a few troops continued to fight for the Spanish. By the end of the year 1821, Mexico was independent from Spain.

7. Mexico's problems didn't end with its independence. The people disagreed over how Mexico should be ruled. Some people wanted another king. In the year 1822, Iturbide took over the new Mexican government by force. He was made **emperor**, which is like a king. But the Mexicans were not happy with Iturbide as their ruler. They turned against him and forced him out of office. In the year 1824, new leaders decided Mexico would be a republic. The people chose Guadalupe Victoria as their first president. He had been a follower of Hidalgo and Morelos.

 REVIEW What kind of government did the new leaders of Mexico decide to have?

The Monroe Doctrine

8. Leaders in the U.S. were aware of revolutions in Central and South America. They were worried about changes in some European governments. Russia, Austria, and Prussia were strong European countries. Each was governed by a king or emperor. These leaders wanted to end all types of **representative** government in Europe. They didn't want people to elect their own leaders. They wanted only royal people to rule. The U.S. worried that the European leaders would

try to end representative governments in the Americas, too.

9. In 1823, President James Monroe presented the **Monroe Doctrine** to the U.S. government. The Monroe Doctrine was a warning to European countries. In it, President Monroe promised to protect independent countries in the Americas from European countries. He declared that no new colonies could be started in the Americas. Monroe also said that colonies already there could not change their borders.

▲ This map shows when colonies in the Americas won their independence. Haiti and the Dominican Republic are now separate countries, but the island was formerly called Hispaniola. Hispaniola was one of the first islands Columbus discovered. Test yourself: Which country was the first to gain its independence—Mexico, Chile, or Cuba?

CHECK THE OBJECTIVE: **Write in your notebook the names of two Hispanic priests who helped Mexico win its independence.**

UNDERSTANDING WHAT YOU HAVE READ

Read the words in the box. Write the word that completes each sentence.

Monroe Doctrine	royalists
republic	representative

1. Mexicans who supported the Spanish king were called

   _____ .

2. In the year 1824, Mexico became a _____ .

3. European rulers wanted to end _____ governments.

4. The _____ protected new countries in the Americas.

Using Primary Sources: The Monroe Doctrine

Here is part of the Monroe Doctrine as President James Monroe presented it to the Congress in the year 1823.

The American continents, by the free and independent condition which they have assumed [taken on] and maintained [kept], are...not to be considered as subjects for future colonization by any European powers...

The citizens of the United States cherish sentiments [feelings]...in favor of the liberty and happiness of their fellow-men on [the European] side of the Atlantic...It is only when our rights are invaded or seriously menaced [threatened] that we...make preparations for our defense. With the movements in this hemisphere [the Americas] we are of necessity more immediately connected...We...declare that we should consider any attempt on their [the Europeans'] part to extend [spread] their system to any portion of this hemisphere as dangerous to our peace and safety...

But with the governments who have declared their independence and maintained it, and whose independence we have...acknowledged [recognized], we could not view any interposition [interference] for the purpose of oppressing them, or controlling...their destiny...in any other light than as...an unfriendly disposition [act] toward the United States...

TEXAS AND ITS INDEPENDENCE

LEARN NEW WORDS

Say each word. Write the word in the sentence.

jury (JOOR-ee)

1. People who decide if a person on trial has broken a law are members of a _____ .

right (RITE)

2. The freedom to do something, such as believing in a religion, is called a _____ .

victory (VIK-tuh-ree)

3. The country that wins the battle, has the _____ .

LEARN A SKILL: Using Maps

You know that a map can help you answer these questions: Where am I? How can I get from place to place? How far away is it? Remember, a **map** is a drawing of a real place.

The first thing to look for when using a map is the title. The title will tell you what is being shown on the map. Look at the map on page 76. Write the title.

_____

Every map has a direction arrow. The arrow tells you that north (N) is toward the top of the map. South (S) is toward the bottom. West (W) is toward the left side and east (E) is toward the right.

Find the direction arrow. Copy it here.

MAKE PREDICTIONS

Read the title and headings. Use them to make predictions.

Put a (✔) mark next to the things you think you will learn about.

_____ when Anglos settled Texas   _____ why settlers went to war

_____ who Spain fought with   _____ how the U.S. freed Mexico

_____ why Anglos were angry   _____ how Texas won its independence

OBJECTIVE: **Read to find out who fought in the battle at the Alamo.**

TIP: **The title and headings will help you.**

Anglos Settle in Mexican Texas

1. In the year 1821, Anglos began moving to Texas. Remember that Texas was part of the republic of Mexico. Some Anglos were given large amounts of land in Texas. These people were called **empresarios** (ehm-preh-SAH-ree-ohs). Many settlers came with the empresarios. They agreed to speak Spanish, become Catholic, and obey Mexican laws. One famous empresario was Stephen Austin. He brought 300 settlers to Texas in 1821.

Anglos in Mexico Are Angry

2. Many of the Anglo settlers had come to Texas with their slaves. In 1829, Mexico declared that **slavery**, the buying and keeping of slaves, was against the law. This made the new settlers angry. They wanted to keep their slaves.

3. There were other things the Anglos did not like about the Mexican government. Mexico did not promise anyone a trial by **jury**. This meant that the government could accuse anyone of breaking a law. The government could arrest and put a person in jail. The government did not have to prove that the person had broken a law. Settlers also wanted certain **rights**, such as freedom to practice any religion. Mexico had no law that promised any rights to the settlers.

 REVIEW

What were some things that the settlers did not like about the Mexican government?

▲ Texans fought Mexico for their independence. This picture shows an important battle that was fought at a place called the Alamo. The battle at the Alamo lasted 12 days. Several thousand Mexicans fought against less than 200 Texans. Finally, the Texans lost. But the name of the Alamo came to stand for the Texans' fight for independence.

4. The settlements in Texas were growing! By the year 1832, Texas had about 30,000 Anglo settlers. More Anglos than Mexicans lived in Texas. The Anglos wanted to live under the laws of the U.S. But Mexico said they had to follow Mexican laws. Then Mexico decided that no more Anglos could move to Texas. This made the settlers angry. Stephen Austin went to Mexico City in 1832 to ask for more freedom for settlers in Texas. Mexico refused. Austin told the settlers to start their own government. The Mexicans then put Austin in jail.

Settlers Go to War with Mexico

5. In the year 1833, Antonio López de Santa Anna (deh SAN-tah AH-nah) was

elected president of Mexico. He **centralized** the government. This gave the government more power to tell people what to do. People in Mexico had less freedom.

6. In the year 1835, fighting began between Texans and the Mexican government. Mexican soldiers tried to take a cannon, or a large gun, from a Texan town. This angered the Texans. Texas fighters attacked and captured the town of San Antonio. In March 1836, President Santa Anna led his army to San Antonio to stop the Texans.

 REREAD What town did the Texans attack and capture?

7. Less than 200 Texans waited for Santa Anna at the **Alamo** (AL-uh-moh). The Alamo had been a mission, but was turned into a fort. Among those at the Alamo were nine Hispanic Texans led by Captain Juan Seguín (seh-GEEN). Santa Anna reached the Alamo with several thousand Mexican soldiers. After 12 days of fighting, Santa Anna won the battle of the Alamo. This battle was a **victory** for Mexico.

Texas Wins its Independence

8. In April 1836, Sam Houston led the Texans in a surprise attack on Santa Anna's troops. The Texans attacked the Mexicans at San Jacinto (san hah-SEEN-toh). As they fought, the Texans shouted "Remember the Alamo!" They won the battle, captured Santa Anna, and had a great victory. The Texans forced Santa Anna to give up Texas.

 LOOK Find San Jacinto on the map on this page. Was this battle a Texan or a Mexican victory? Hint: use the map key.

9. Texas became an independent republic. Texans no longer had to obey the Mexican government. Although Mexico refused to admit that Texas was a new, free republic, the United States did.

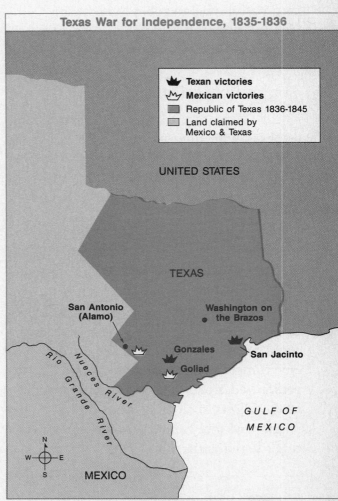

▲ This map shows the republic of Texas when it won its freedom from Mexico in the year 1836. Remember that fighting began when Mexican soldiers tried to take a cannon from a Texan town. This town was Gonzales. Find it on the map. Then test yourself: Who had the victory at Gonzales? Use your map key for help.

CHECK THE OBJECTIVE: Write in your notebook a sentence that tells who fought in the battle at the Alamo.

UNDERSTANDING WHAT YOU HAVE READ

Read. Write the letter to match.

_____ 1. Stephen Austin

_____ 2. empresarios

_____ 3. the Alamo

_____ 4. Juan Seguín

_____ 5. Sam Houston

_____ 6. Santa Anna

a. famous battle lost to Mexico

b. man who went to jail after telling settlers to start their own government

c. Anglos who were given large pieces of land

d. led a surprise attack on Santa Anna

e. president of Mexico

f. led Hispanics at the Alamo

Spotlight on People: Lorenzo de Zavala

Lorenzo de Zavala (deh sah-VAH-lah) was a Mexican government official. Zavala did not agree with the ideas of Santa Anna, Mexico's new president. He joined the Texas settlers in their fight for independence. Zavala signed the Texas Declaration of Independence. In March 1836, he became the first vice president of the Republic of Texas. Zavala even designed the first flag for the new Texas republic. He died in the year 1836.

Zavala wrote several books on Mexican history. His granddaughter later fought to save historical places in Texas. She helped to protect the Alamo building, an important part of Texan history.

▲ Lorenzo de Zavala was the first vice president of the Republic of Texas.

THE WAR BETWEEN MEXICO AND THE U.S.

LEARN NEW WORDS

Say each word. Write the word in the sentence.

citizen (SIT-uh-zun)

1. A person who is born in, or who chooses to live in a country is a _____ of that country.

argue (ARE-gyoo)

2. When two people, or countries, disagree about something, they may _____ .

defeat (dih-FEET)

3. To win a victory over your enemies is to _____ them.

LEARN A SKILL: Taking Notes

Taking notes can help you remember what you read. Follow these steps:

- Turn headings into questions.

- Read the lesson.

- Write the answer to each questions.

Read paragraph 6 on page 79. To take good notes, follow the three steps.

Question: _____

Answer/notes: _____

_____

_____

_____

MAKE PREDICTIONS

Read the title and heading. Use them to make predictions.

Put a (✔) mark next to the things you think you will learn about.

_____ how Mexicans lived in Texas

_____ who disagreed over borders

_____ the jewelry Mexicans wore

_____ when war with Mexico began

_____ where cowboys lived in Texas

_____ when a treaty was signed

Anglos and Mexicans in Texas

1. What happened to the Mexicans living in Texas after it got its independence? Mexicans were told they could stay in Texas and become Texas **citizens**. If they stayed, Mexicans were promised the same rights as Anglo citizens had. Mexicans were also told that they could own land, just as Anglo citizens could.

2. Not all Anglos kept this promise. Some Anglo Texans tried to make the Mexicans move south of the Rio Grande River. Even Juan Seguín was forced to move south. He was a Hispanic who had fought for the independence of Texas.

Disagreements Over Borders

3. By the year 1845, Texas had been independent for about 10 years. During that time, there were disagreements between Texas and Mexico. Then Texas became the 28th state to join the United States of America. Mexico was angry when Texas joined the United States. Mexico wanted nothing to do with the U.S. now.

4. Then Mexico and the United States started to **argue** about their borders. Mexico said the border of Texas was at the Nueces River. The United States said it was farther to the south, at the Rio Grande. Both claimed the land between the two rivers.

What can you do when you and a friend argue over who owns something you both found? Talk about it with your teacher.

5. In April 1846, American troops marched into the land between the Nueces and Rio Grande Rivers. They were led by Major General Zachary Taylor. Mexican troops crossed the Rio Grande to stop the Americans. The two armies fought. The Mexicans forced the Americans back. The U.S. was **defeated** in this battle.

Look at the map on page 76. Find the two rivers that formed borders that the U.S. and Mexico argued about.

War With Mexico

6. The U.S. declared war on Mexico in May 1846. This was not just because the U.S. had been defeated by Mexico. The U.S. wanted the land between the two rivers, along with other land. The U.S. asked Mexico to sell the land. Mexico refused.

▲ This picture shows a battle during the U.S. War with Mexico. Young soldiers, called "Los Niños" became heroes trying to defend the castle.

7. Major General Taylor led U.S. troops across the Rio Grande. He defeated the Mexicans in important battles at Monterrey and Buena Vista. He became an American hero, and later was elected president of the U.S.

8. The war was not only near the Texas border. In the Southwest, General Stephen W. Kearney led a group of Americans to California. California was still part of Mexico. Kearney found that some American soldiers had already set up a republic. They called this new republic the Bear Flag Republic.

 REREAD Who ruled California when the Mexican War was started?

9. In March 1847, U.S. General Winfield Scott led an army by sea to the Mexican port of Veracruz. By May, Scott captured both Veracruz and Mexico City, the capital. The Mexican War ended soon after those two U.S. victories.

A Treaty Is Signed

10. In February 1848, Mexico and the United States signed a treaty to end the war. This was called the **Treaty of Guadalupe Hidalgo**. In the treaty, Mexico agreed to sell land to the United States. This land was called the **Mexican Cession**. It included California, Nevada, and Utah, along with parts of New Mexico, Arizona, Wyoming, and Colorado. The United States paid Mexico $15 million for the land. The treaty also promised Mexicans living in the Southwest U.S. the same rights as American citizens.

 REVIEW What did Mexico and the United States agree to at the end of the Mexican War?

11. Many Anglos did not obey the treaty. Mexicans lost their rights and much of their land to the Anglos. Mexicans could not get fair trials. Some Mexican people were even **lynched** by the Anglos. A lynching is when an angry group of people kills someone hated by the group.

12. The Mexican War had important results for the United States. The U.S. gained a lot of land in the Mexican Cession. But there were problems. In the next lesson, you will learn that slavery was one of these problems.

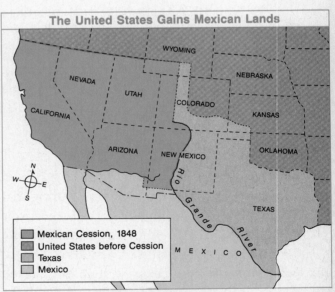

▲ This map shows the lands gained by the United States from Mexico in the Mexican Cession. The new southern border of Texas was at the Rio Grande River. Test yourself: How many states, or parts of states, did the U.S. gain in the Treaty of Guadalupe Hidalgo?

CHECK THE OBJECTIVE: Write down in your notebook one reason why the United States and Mexico fought the Mexican War.

UNDERSTANDING WHAT YOU HAVE READ

Read each pair of sentences. Underline the sentence that is true.

1. After Texas independence, Mexicans could become Texas citizens.
   Mexicans were not allowed to be citizens after Texas independence.

2. The U.S. and Mexico agreed about the Texas border between them.
   The U.S. and Mexico disagreed about the Texas border between them.

3. Mexico declared war on the United States.
   The United States declared war on Mexico.

4. A treaty promised Mexicans in the U.S. the same rights as U.S. citizens.
   A treaty said Mexicans in the U.S. could not have the same rights as U.S. citizens.

Using Primary Sources: The Treaty of Guadalupe Hidalgo

Mexico and the U.S. signed the **Treaty of Guadalupe Hidalgo** (GWAH-dah-loo-peh ee-DAHL-goh) on February 2, 1848, to end the Mexican War.

> ARTICLE VIII Mexicans now established [living] in territories previously belonging to Mexico, and which remain for the future within the limits of the United States . . . shall be free to continue where they now reside [live], or to remove [move] at any time to the Mexican republic, retaining [keeping] the property which they possess . . . or disposing [selling the property] and removing the proceeds [money gained from a sale] wherever they please, without their being subject . . . to any contribution, tax, or charge whatever . . .
>
> ARTICLE IX [These people are guaranteed] the enjoyment of all the rights of citizens of the United States according to the principles of the Constitution; and in the meantime shall be maintained and protected in the free enjoyment of their liberty and property, and . . . in the free exercise of their religion . . .

HISPANICS IN THE CIVIL WAR

LEARN NEW WORDS

Say each word. Write the word in the sentence.

regiment (REJ-uh-munt)

rank (RANK)

apprentice (uh-PRENT-us)

1. A large group of soldiers in an army is called a

   _____ .

2. The level or grade of a soldier is called a _____ .

3. Someone who learns a skill or a job from an experienced person is called an _____ .

LEARN A SKILL: Summarizing

When you **summarize**, you tell about the most important ideas. These important ideas are called main ideas. You can find main ideas by looking at headings. You can also look for the main idea sentence in a paragraph. Headings and main idea sentences can help you write a summary.

Remember these two things when you write a summary.

> • A summary should give the main ideas.
>
> • A summary is very short.

When you finish reading "The Civil War," come back to this page. Work with a classmate to write a summary. (Remember to use the headings.)

_____

_____

_____

_____

MAKE PREDICTIONS

Read the title and headings. Use them to make predictions.

Put a (✔) mark next to the things you think you will learn about.

_____ what happened before the war   _____ who won the War of 1812

_____ when the Civil War began   _____ why Farragut was a hero

_____ which Hispanics fought in the war   _____ what crops grew in the South

OBJECTIVE: Read to learn ways Hispanic Americans helped fight the U. S. Civil War.

TIP: Taking notes as you read will help you.

Before the Civil War

1. New lands in the Southwest were added to the United States during the mid-1800s. The U.S. leaders had to decide whether to allow slavery in the Southwest. Slavery was still allowed in the South, but not in the North.

2. In the U.S. Congress, the officials could not agree about slavery. They could not agree about taxes either. Finally, some southern states decided to leave the United States. These states formed their own country. They called it the Confederate States of America, or the **Confederacy** (kun-FED-uh-ruh-see). More southern states joined the Confederacy. Soon there would be a war between southern and northern states.

Look at the map on page 84. Find the states that joined the Confederacy. How many Confederate states were there? Name one. Use the map key to help you.

The Civil War Begins

3. In 1861, the **Civil War** began in the U.S. In a civil war, two groups from the same country fight one another. In the U.S. Civil War, citizens from the North and the South fought each other. Even friends and brothers fought each other, when they were on opposite sides. The war lasted until 1865.

4. Almost 10,000 Hispanic Americans fought in the Civil War. Hispanics chose sides according to what they believed or where they

▲ David Farragut captured Mobile, Alabama, for the Union. The U.S. Congress gave Farragut the rank of admiral of the navy. He was the first person to be given this high rank.

lived. Some fought for the Confederacy. Others fought for the northern states, or the **Union**. In some **regiments**, the soldiers were Hispanic, and they were led by Hispanic officers. In other regiments, the Hispanics fought alongside other American soldiers.

How did Hispanics choose which side of the Civil War to support? Hint: The second sentence in paragraph 4 tells you.

Hispanics Fight in the War

5. In March 1862, José Francisco Chaves (SHAH-vehs) fought in the Battle of Glorieta Pass. He was a Hispanic officer in the Union Army. Chaves helped the Union capture land from the Confederates. The land was near Albuquerque and Santa Fe, in New Mexico.

6. During the Civil War, Santos Benavides (beh-nah-VEE-des) held the highest **rank** in the Confederate Army. In March 1864, Benavides led his regiment against the Union troops attacking Brownsville Texas. It was a victory for the Confederates.

7. Loretta Velásquez (veh-LAHS-kehs), a woman from Cuba, wanted to help the Confederacy. In the year 1860, she pretended to be a man and joined the Confederate Army. She fought in several battles before anyone found out she was a woman.

8. Federico Fernández Cavada (kuh-VAH-dah) was a soldier in the Union Army. He also was from Cuba. Cavada was put in charge of the Union's hot-air balloons.

Farragut Is a Hero

9. The most famous Hispanic American in the Civil War was David Farragut. Farragut fought in the War of 1812 when he was a young boy. He was an **apprentice** to a captain in the U.S. Navy. Farragut fought on the Union side in the Civil War.

10. In the year 1862, Farragut captured two New Orleans forts. He attacked the forts at night and defeated the Confederate ships protecting the forts. Then Farragut captured important Confederate forts along the Mississippi River. He helped stop the enemy from getting supplies. Farragut also helped stop enemy messages from being passed along the river.

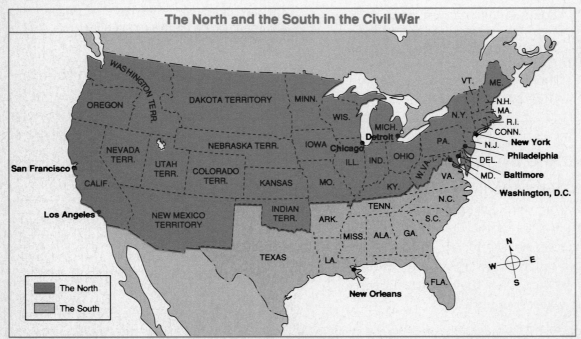

The North and the South in the Civil War

▲ During the Civil War, the North and the South fought each other. Some Hispanic Americans fought on the Union side (the North). Other Hispanic Americans fought on the side of the Confederacy (the South).

CHECK THE OBJECTIVE: Write down in your notebook two ways that Hispanic Americans helped fight the Civil War.

UNDERSTANDING WHAT YOU HAVE READ

Find the correct answer to each question. Circle the letter.

1. What problems led to the Civil War?
   a. problems about a new president
   b. problems about slavery and taxes
   c. problems about trading with Mexico

2. What two sides fought the Civil War?
   a. the Confederacy and the Union
   b. the Union and the North
   c. the Confederacy and the South

3. Hispanics fought
   a. for the South.
   b. for the Union and the Confederacy.
   c. for the North.

4. Loretta Velásquez pretended to be a man
   a. to sail in the navy.
   b. to go up in a balloon.
   c. to fight in the army.

Spotlight on People: David Farragut

David Farragut was born in the year 1801 in Tennessee. He was the son of Jorge Ferragut, a hero of the American Revolution. (Ferragut changed his last name to Farragut after the revolution.) Farragut fought in the Civil War. He is probably best known for capturing Mobile, Alabama.

In August 1864, he led a group of wooden ships into Mobile Bay. With the ships were four submarines. The Confederates had placed many torpedoes in the bay. Back then, a torpedo was a type of bomb that exploded when hit by something. One of Farragut's submarines hit a torpedo and exploded. Then Farragut moved his own ship forward to lead the group. He shouted, "Damn the torpedoes! Full steam ahead!" No more torpedoes exploded. Farragut's ships entered the bay safely. His men battled the Confederate enemy and won. Mobile was soon captured for the Union. The U.S. Congress gave Farragut the high rank of admiral to honor him.

▲ David Farragut was a navy admiral.

REVIEW 4

SUMMARY OF LESSONS 14-19

Here are some important ideas you learned in Lessons 14-19. Write the one you want to remember.

- Mestizos, mulatos, and criollos are all Hispanic. (14)

- Florida became part of the U.S. in 1821, when Spain signed the Adams-Onís Treaty. (15)

- Mexico won its independence from Spain in 1821, after 11 years of struggle. (16)

- In 1836, Sam Houston led the battle that freed Texas from Mexico. (17)

- In 1848, the Treaty of Guadalupe Hidalgo ended the Mexican War and made California, Nevada, Utah, and other lands part of the U.S. (18)

- Hispanic Americans fought on both sides in the U.S. Civil War. (19)

REVIEWING NEW WORDS

Look up the words below in the Glossary. Write the correct word in each sentence.

citizen (18)	treaty (14)	right (17)
revolution (16)	rank (19)	border (15)

1. When Texas became independent, each Mexican living there could choose to become a Texas _____ .

2. During the Mexican War, the U.S. and Mexico fought over the _____ between their countries.

3. A _____ is a fight to overthrow a government or a country.

4. Santos Benavides held the highest _____ of any Hispanic Confederate officer.

5. Each citizen in the U.S. has the _____ to vote.

6. Great Britain and the U.S. signed a _____ to end the war.

REVIEWING WHAT YOU HAVE READ

Read. Write the letter to match.

_____ 1. Monroe Doctrine

_____ 2. Seminoles

_____ 3. David Farragut

a. the most famous Hispanic American in the Civil War

b. a promise by the U.S. to protect new countries in the Americas

c. Native Americans who fought for their land by attacking settlers

_____ 4. the Alamo

_____ 5. Hispanics

_____ 6. Mexican Cession

d. people who speak Spanish and have Spanish traditions

e. the land Mexico sold to the U.S. after the Mexican War

f. a famous place where Texans lost a battle for independence from Mexico

REVIEWING SKILLS

Study the time line.

Read. Write the correct date next to the event.

_____ The Civil War begins

_____ The Monroe Doctrine is presented

_____ Texas becomes independent

_____ The Civil War ends

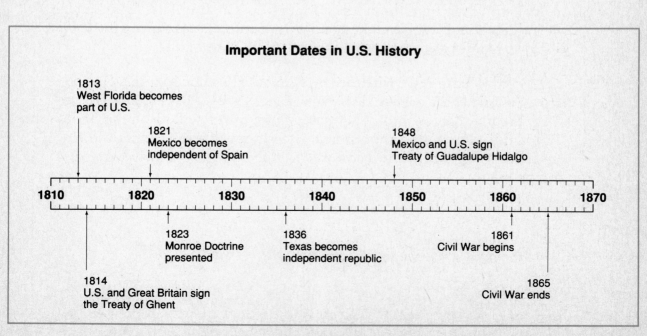

Important Dates in U.S. History

1813
West Florida becomes
part of U.S.

1821
Mexico becomes
independent of Spain

1848
Mexico and U.S. sign
Treaty of Guadalupe Hidalgo

1810   1820   1830   1840   1850   1860   1870

1823
Monroe Doctrine
presented

1836
Texas becomes
independent republic

1861
Civil War begins

1814
U.S. and Great Britain sign
the Treaty of Ghent

1865
Civil War ends

CONCLUSION

What have we learned about the history of Hispanic Americans in the U.S.? We have learned that nearly 500 years ago, brave explorers from Spain began coming to the New World looking for new lands and great riches. We learned that Spanish explorers, or conquistadores, were the first Europeans to discover the Grand Canyon, to cross the Mississippi River, and to reach the Pacific coast of the U.S.

These conquistadores started many small settlements, or pueblos, in the southwestern part of the U.S. Many of these settlements, such as St. Augustine, in Florida, have become large American cities. When Spanish settlers came to the New World, they changed the lives of the Native Americans. Missionaries came to teach Native Americans about Christianity. Priests taught Native Americans how to read and write, too. However, the Spanish settlers also forced many Native Americans to work for them.

The Spanish explored and settled the New World for many years. During those years, the settlers brought their Spanish language, customs, and traditions to the New World. Hispanics have contributed many things that are part of our everyday lives. Today we can see many houses built in the Spanish style in America. Many animals, such as horses and cattle, were brought to America by Spanish settlers. The Spanish also brought new crops to the New World.

Hispanic Americans have helped to make America the strong country that it is today. Hispanics, like Jorge Ferragut, helped the colonists in their fight for independence from Great Britain. Years later, Ferragut's son, David, fought against the Confederates during the Civil War. Hispanics also supported the U.S. in the War of 1812.

In Volume B, we will learn more about Hispanic American history from 1865 up to the present day. We will learn about Hispanic Americans who became heroes in other American wars. We will also read about Hispanics who became important in American politics, business, the arts, and sports. We will find out how much Hispanics have contributed to the American way of life.

GLOSSARY

Alamo: a mission where a famous battle was fought during the Texas war for independence (p. 76)

ancestors: the people in a family who lived and died long ago (p.63)

Anglos: English-speaking, non-Hispanic Americans (p. 63)

apprentice: someone who learns a job from a skilled person (p. 84)

argue: to fight or disagree about something (p. 79)

Asia: the largest of the seven continents, or land masses, on earth; its borders extend from Europe and Africa in the west to the Pacific Ocean in the east (p. 5)

battle: a fight in a war (p. 64)

border: the line that divides two areas of land (p. 67)

capture: to take something or someone by force and gain control (p. 53)

centralized: put under the control of a central power (p. 76)

citizen: a person who is born in a country, or who chooses to live in a country, and follow its laws (p. 79)

Civil War: the war between the North and the South in the U.S. from 1861-1865 (p. 83)

claim: to say you own something; to demand or ask for something (p. 9)

class system: a system in which a person's importance is based on family background (p.50)

coast: the land along the ocean (p. 9)

colonies: settlements that people from one land build in another land (p. 17)

colonists: people who settled in colonies (p. 17)

community: a group of people living near each other (p. 49)

Confederacy: the southern states, or the South, during the Civil War (p. 83)

Congress: the part of the U.S. government that makes laws (p. 69)

conquer: to fight and win control over a land and its people (p. 9)

conqueror: someone who fights and wins control over a land and its people (p. 14)

convert: to change a person's religious beliefs (p. 27)

culture: language, arts, customs, and beliefs of a people (p. 49)

customs: practices or habits that most people in a group or country usually follow (p. 49)

declare: to state something officially; when a country declares war on another country, it is making the war official (p. 54)

defeat: to win a victory over an enemy (p. 79)

depot: a place where people from an army are trained; a place where guns and other supplies are kept (p. 57)

desert: an area of land that has very little or no rainfall (p. 45)

duties: taxes (p. 41)

emperor: the ruler of an empire (p. 72)

empire: a group of nations or lands ruled by one government or ruler (p. 13)

Europe: a continent that extends from the Atlantic Ocean to Asia (p. 5)

European: a person who comes from Europe (p. 9)

explorer: a person who looks for new lands (p. 9)

filigree: a lacy design often used in making fine jewelry (p. 65)

fort: a place where soldiers live; it is built large and strong to keep enemies out (p. 24)

founded: when the first steps are taken to set up or build something new, such as a city or a building (p. 27)

glacier: a large area of ice (p. 46)

goods: things that can be bought and sold (p. 5)

government: a way of ruling a group of people or a country (p. 27)

Hispanic: a person who probably speaks Spanish or has Spanish background and traditions (p. 63)

Hispaniola: an island between Cuba and Puerto Rico; today the island is known as Haiti and the Dominican Republic (p. 6)

independence: having freedom from the rule of others (p. 32)

integrated: brought together; an area that is integrated is made open to people of all races (p. 58)

invade: to enter a country in order to conquer it (p. 31)

island: an area of land with water on all sides (p. 6)

jury: a group of 12 people chosen to decide a court case (p. 75)

language: the words we use to speak or write (p. 49)

Louisiana Purchase: a large area of land in the U.S. bought from France in 1803 (p. 42)

lynch: when an angry group of people illegally kill someone hated by the group (p. 80)

merchant: a person who buys and sells goods (p. 5)

Mexican Cession: land Mexico was forced to sell to the U.S. after the Mexican War in 1848 (p. 80)

mining: digging metals from the ground (p. 17)

mission: a church or place where the Christian religion was taught, often to Native Americans (p. 18)

missionaries: people sent by the Roman Catholic Church to teach the Christian religion to the people of the New World (p. 9)

Monroe Doctrine: a U.S. promise to protect countries in the Americas from further European settlement (p. 72)

mouth: place where a river enters a larger body of water, such as the ocean (p. 42)

nations: countries (p. 35)

Native Americans: the first people to live in the New World (p. 10)

New World: the area of land that includes North, South, and Central America (p. 6)

ocean: a large body of water that covers a large part the earth's surface (p. 5)

official: something that is done according to rules or laws; a person holding a government job (p. 41)

peninsula: land with water on three sides (p. 35)

permanent: something made to last a long time (p. 24)

port: a place along a coast where ships load and unload (p. 53)

priests: religious Christian men who work for the Catholic Church (p. 18)

purchase: something that is bought; to buy something (p. 67)

range: an open area of land where animals live and feed (p. 58)

rank: the level or grade of a soldier (p. 83)

rebellion: a fight against rulers or a government (p. 28)

record: something that is written down and kept (p. 46)

regiment: a large group, or troops, of soldiers in an army (p. 83)

region: large areas of land (p. 35)

religion: the spiritual beliefs of a people (p. 7)

representative: a word describing a type of government in which officials make decisions for the people who elected them (p. 72)

republic: a form of government where the authority belongs to the people; the people vote for leaders to run the government (p. 67)

revolution: a fight for independence or change; the result may be a new government (p. 71)

right: the freedom to do something, such as vote or worship, as you please (p. 75)

route: the way to go by land or by water (p. 5)

royalists: supporters of a royal family as government leaders (p. 71)

ruins: the remains of a place that has been destroyed (p. 31)

ruler: the leader of a country or empire (p. 13)

San Salvador: the island near Cuba on which Columbus first landed (p. 6)

Secretary of State: a U.S. government leader (p. 68)

secularization: making something that has been connected to religion not religious anymore (p. 36)

Secularization Act: a Mexican law that took mission lands away from the control of the Catholic Church (p. 36)

Sephardic: the Hebrew word for "Spain"; Sephardic Jews left Spain in 1492 rather than be forced to become Christians (p. 63)

settlement: a new place set up for settlers (p. 23)

settlers: the first people to move to, and live in, a new place (p. 24)

Seven Cities of Gold: cities supposed to be filled with gold that the Spanish explorers searched for, but never found, in the Southwest (p. 10)

slave: a person who is forced to work for others without being paid for the work (p. 17)

slavery: the buying, selling, and keeping of slaves (p. 75)

soldiers: people who serve in a country's army in order to protect the country (p. 24)

Spain: a country in western Europe (p. 5)

strait: a waterway joining two large bodies of water (p. 46)

taxes: money paid by citizens to their government to run the country (p. 17)

territory: a large area of land held by a ruler or a nation (p. 41)

traditions: customs or accepted ways of doing things (p. 63)

treasure fleets: groups of ships that carried silver from the New World to Spain (p. 18)

treaty: a formal agreement between two countries, usually signed to end a war (p. 64)

Treaty of Guadalupe Hidalgo: treaty signed by the U.S. and Mexico in 1848 to end the Mexican War (p. 80)

trial: a hearing; in a trial, evidence about a crime is presented in court to a judge and a jury (p. 68)

tribute: a kind of tax; during the 1600s, Native Americans paid tribute to the Spanish in corn, cloth, or work (p. 28)

troop: a group of soldiers; part of a regiment (p. 41)

Union: the northern states, or the North, during the Civil War (p. 83)

victory: winning over an enemy in a war or battle (p. 76)

weapons: things used to fight, such as guns and knives (p. 68)

SPANISH WORD GLOSSARY

adelantado (ah-deh-lahn-TAH-doh): governor (p. 23)
adobe (ah-DOH-beh): a brick-like material made by drying a mixture of mud and straw in the sun (p. 27)

cabildo (kah-BEEL-doh): town council (p. 27)
conquistadores (kon-KEES-tah-dor-ehs): conquerors (p. 9)
criollos (kree-OH-yohs): children born in the Americas to Spanish parents (p. 50)

empresarios (ehm-preh-SAH-ree-ohs): Anglo settlers who were given land in the Mexican state of Texas (p. 75)
encomenderos (en-koh-men-DEH-rohs): early Spanish colonists who owned encomiendas, or large areas of land, in the New World (p. 17)
encomiendas (en-koh-mee-EN-dahs): large areas of land in the New World, given to Spanish colonists by the king of Spain (p. 17)

fandango (fan-DAHN-goh): a popular Spanish dance from the 1800s (p. 63)

hidalgos (ee-DAHL-gohs): Spanish gentlemen (p. 32)
Hispanico (ee-SPAH-nee-koh): a person who probably speaks Spanish or has Spanish background and traditions (p. 63)

Ladino (lah-DEE-noh): a language similar to Spanish, spoken by Sephardic Jews (p. 63)
Latino (lah-TEE-noh): a Hispanic person (p. 63)

mestizos (meh-STEE-sohs): people with both Spanish and Native American backgrounds (p. 50)
mulatos (muh-LAH-tohs): people with both European and African backgrounds (p. 64)

peninsulares (peh-NEEN-soo-lah-res): people born in Spain of Spanish parents (p. 50)
presidios (preh-SEE-dyohs): Spanish military forts (p. 32)
pueblos (PWEH-blohs): towns where Native Americans and Spanish settlers lived in the Southwest (p. 28)

rancheros (rahn-CHEH-rohs): ranchers who owned large areas of land (p. 36)
ranchos (RAHN-chohs): ranches, or big areas of land, often used to raise cattle or sheep (p. 36)
rebozo (reh-BOH-soh): a long shawl of fine cloth (p. 47)
rodeo (roh-DEH-oh): a contest in which cowboys, or vaqueros, ride horses and rope cattle (p. 58)

sarape (sah-RAH-peh): a many-colored blanket worn over one shoulder (p. 47)

vaqueros (vah-KEH-rohs): Spanish cowboys in the Southwest (p. 36)

INDEX